ANABAPTISM IN FLANDERS, 1530-1650

ANABAPTISM IN FLANDERS
1530-1650
A Century of Struggle

BY A. L. E. VERHEYDEN

Laureate of the Royal Academy of Belgium

WIPF & STOCK · Eugene, Oregon

To My Spiritual Kinsmen in America

I am confident that many of my readers are already well acquainted with the history of Dutch Anabaptism. The writing of church history has, however, ignored almost completely the heroic struggle of the stalwart Flemings who stood for this same faith.

Many a historian concedes to Flemish Anabaptism a life of barely twenty-five or thirty years—a luxuriant growth which was doomed to perish as soon as the storms came. But the reality was quite different. Chronologically, Anabaptism was alive in Flanders from 1530 until the middle of the seventeenth century. Numerically it won a larger following than Lutheranism and for long years kept pace with Calvinism. It was Anabaptists who wrote their testimony of blood on the pages, rich with martyrs, of the history of the Reformation in our land. In this tiny province they did not count life too dear a price for Christian fidelity.

It is to the overseas successors of these martyrs that this book is dedicated. May it help them to see the tenacity with which their faith was defended in Flanders.

Vilvoorde, December 17, 1946
A. L. E. Verheyden

Wipf and Stock Publishers
199 W 8th Ave, Suite 3
Eugene, OR 97401

Anabaptism in Flanders 1530 - 1650
By Verheyden, A. L. E.
Copyright©1961 Herald Press
ISBN 13: 978-1-5326-6700-8
Publication date 12/03/2008
Previously published by Herald Press, 1961

PREFACE

One of the very few serious historians studying the Belgian Reformation, Dr. A. L. E. Verheyden, formerly Lecturer in History at the University of Liége, now Professor of History in the Academy at Aalst, has devoted long years of painstaking study to the reconstruction of the history of Anabaptism in his country. Beginning with exhaustive local martyrological studies (Bruges in 1944, Ghent in 1946, Courtrai and Brussels in 1950, synthesized for popular readership in *Le Martyrologe Protestant des Pays-Bas du Sud* . . . 1960), and numerous articles in the *Bulletin de la Societe d'Histoire du Protestantisme Belge,* and the *Bulletin de la Commission Royal d'Histoire,* he has moved on to synthesize his data on the provincial level (*Doopsgezinden te Ghent,* 1943; but especially in the present work, dating from 1946) and, more recently, for all the Southern Netherlands, i.e., today's Belgium. His *Geschiedenis der Doopsgezinden in de zuidelijke Nederlanden in de XVIe Eeuw* (Brussels, 1959) earned for him the title of Laureate of the Royal Academy. This recent work includes within its broader treatment the main lines of the history of Anabaptism in Flanders, those now being published in the present volume, but with less detailed documentation.

Beyond his interest in Anabaptist studies Professor Verheyden is a respected authority on other aspects of Reformation history. His *Le Bilan du Conseil des Troubles* (Royal Academy, 1960) recounts one of the darkest chapters of the history of religious repression in Europe. His *De Hervorming in de zuidelijke Nederlanden in de XVIe Eeuw* (Brussels, 1949), an official publication of the national Belgian Protestant Synod, was the first Reformation history in Belgium to describe fairly the place of Anabaptism in the early decades of the Reformation.

The present volume offers the first comprehensive study of Anabaptism in Flanders in the sixteenth century. Based upon a massive use of the sources, it is thorough, completely objective and fair, and exhaustive. The picture it presents is a new one in its evidence of the surprising extent of the spread of the movement geographically, as well as its depth and tenacity in the face of the severest persecution. That Anabaptism persisted in Flanders almost a half century beyond 1600 was not clearly known before. That apart from certain aberrations at the very beginning Flemish Anabaptism was completely peaceful, nonresistant, and evangelical, largely after the pattern of Menno Simons, is irrefutably demonstrated. A major gap in our knowledge and understanding of continental Anabaptism has now been closed in an exceptionally competent fashion by a master in the field.

The editors and publishers owe an apology to the author for the late appearance of the volume. The manuscript was submitted originally in 1947. Part of the delay in its publication has been due to the delay in completing the translation from the Flemish into the English. The translation in its present form is the combined work of three persons, two from Holland, namely, Miss Meintje Kuitse of Amsterdam and Jan Matthijssen of Meppel, and John Howard Yoder of Elkhart, Indiana. The former two did their work while exchange students at Goshen College. Mr. Yoder revised the entire manuscript, in consultation with the author, in 1959. To all of these hearty appreciation is due, as well as to Elizabeth Horsch Bender for her copy editing. Mr. Lewis Martin of Harrisonburg, Virginia, generously contributed to the cost of the translation.

For the Mennonite Historical Society
Harold S. Bender, Editor

TRANSLATOR'S PREFACE

The use of hereditary surnames was not yet established in Flanders in the period covered by this study; most of the persons named bear surnames designating their own profession or place of origin or that of the father. These surnames have generally not been translated. Similarly most place names have been left in the original tongue.

Dr. Verheyden's writing presupposes an awareness of the main outlines of the history of the Netherlands in the sixteenth century. To orient the reader for whom his allusions to historical events and personages might not be understandable, a chronological table of the principal events of the period has been provided (page xvf). A map of Flanders will be found on page xvi. Works and archival sources to which frequent reference is made are indicated in the footnotes by abbreviated titles; a list of works thus referred to will be found on page xiii.

CONTENTS

KEY TO BIBLIOGRAPHICAL ABBREVIATIONS

I. ARCHIVAL SOURCES

For archival sources the name of the collection of documents is italicized; only this part of the reference is ever abbreviated, and only such references are indicated here as have appeared frequently enough to be abbreviated. References from the Bruges Archives (City and State) and from Courtrai (City) are given in full.

Brussels Royal, *EA*	*Etats-Audiences*
Ghent City, *Crime*	*Bouc van den Crime*
Ghent City, *KR*	*Keure-Resolutien*
Ghent State: *RVSC*	*Raad van Vlaanderen, Secrete Camere*
RVBW	*Raad van Vlaanderen, Briefwisseling*
RVSF	*Raad van Vlaanderen, Serie F*

II. PRINTED SOURCES

B.R.N.	*Bibliotheca Reformatoria Neerlandica* (The Hague, 1908 ff.)
B.C.R.H.	*Bulletin de la Commission Royale d'Histoire de Belgique* (Brussels, 1834 ff.; fourth series 1920 ff.)
van Braght, *Mirror*	Tieleman van Braght, *Het Bloedig Tooneel of Martelaers Spiegel der Doopsgezinde of Weerloose Christenen* (second edition, Amsterdam, 1685)
Broer Cornelis	*Historie van Broer Cornelis Adriaens* (Bruges?, 1640)
de Coussemaker, *Troubles*	Edmond de Coussemaker, *Les Troubles Religieux du XVIᵉ Siècle dans la Flandre Maritime, 1560-1570* (Bruges, 1876)
Génard, *AA*	P. Génard, articles in *Antwerpsch Archievenblad* (Antwerp, 1867-1921, new series 1926 ff.)

de Jonghe, *Ghent*	Bernardus de Jonghe, *Ghendtsche geschiedenissen by forme van maendtregister* (Ghent, 1746)
Menno, *Complete Writings*	John Christian Wenger, ed., *The Complete Writings of Menno Simons, c.1496-1561* (Scottdale, 1956)
Meulman Collection	Ghent University Library, Meulman Collection, with catalog numbers as assigned by J. K. van der Wulp, *Catalogus van de Tractaten . . . I* (Amsterdam, 1866)
van Vaerniwyck, *Van die beroerlicke tijden*	Marcus van Vaerniwyck, *Van die Beroerlicke Tijden in de Nederlanden en voornamelijk in Ghendt, 1566-1568* (Ghent, 5 vol., 1872-1881)
Verheyden, *Bruges*	A. L. E. Verheyden, *Het Brugsch Martyrologium* (Brussels, 1944)
Verheyden, *DtG*	"De Doopsgezinden te Gent (1530-1630)," *Bulletin der Maatschappij voor Oudheidkunde en Geschiedenis,* 1943, 99 ff.
Verheyden, *Ghent*	A. L. E. Verheyden, *Het Gentsche Martyrologium* (Brussels, 1944)
Vos, *DtA*	Karel Vos, "De Doopsgezinden te Antwerpen in de zestiende eeuw," *B.C.R.H.,* LXXXIV (1920), pp. 317-90
V. P., *Successio*	*Successio Anabaptistica* (Cologne, 1603; cf. *Mennonite Encyclopedia,* II, p. 759)

CALENDAR OF PRINCIPAL DATES
IN FLEMISH REFORMATION HISTORY

1521   First edict against the Lutherans, authorizing the death penalty.

1522   (April 23): Frans van der Hulst designated as Inquisitor General to take charge of the battle against heresy in the Netherlands.

1523   (July 1): Henri Voes and Jan van Essen burned at Brussels as (Lutheran) heretics.

1529   First appearance of Anabaptism in the Netherlands.

1545   First appearance of Calvinism in Walloon (French-speaking) territory. First general assembly of representatives of the Mennonite congregations of Flanders.

1550   Appearance of Calvinism in Flemish territory. April 28, a new edict against heresy.

1556   Philip II succeeds Charles V as King of Spain, inaugurating a period of extreme repression.

1559   Philip leaves for Spain, leaving as regent his half-sister, Margaret of Austria, Duchess of Parma.

1565   Formation at Brussels of the Confederation of Nobles, with the aim of obtaining the suspension of the Inquisition and the modification of the edicts against heresy.

1566   (April 5): The nobles present their request to Margaret of Austria. (August): "The Iconoclasm"; a wave of anti-Catholic violence, beginning August 11 in the region of Armentières and Hondschoote, moving northward to Ypres (August 14), Audenaarde (18), Antwerp (20), Ghent (23), Tournai (23), and on through Zeeland and Holland to Friesland, reaching Leeuwarden in September. Calvinists take possession of some church buildings and hold public worship services on a basis of Protestant-Catholic tolerance. Period referred to as "The Wonder Year."

1567   (August 9): The troops of the Duke of Alva, who had replaced Margaret of Austria as Governor General, enter Brussels, restoring Catholic authority in the Southern Netherlands. The northern provinces remain unsubmissive.

(September 5): Formation of the "Conseil des Troubles," created independently of the existing governmental framework, responsible for restoring the Catholic faith and royal authority by extreme repression. Known popularly as the "Blood Council," it was to pronounce 12,000 sentences of death or banishment.

1572 Military expedition of Alva against the northern provinces.

1573 (December 18): Alva is replaced as Governor General by Luis de Zuniga y Requescens, who is instructed by Philip II to be milder in method but to make no concessions.

1576 (November 8): The "Pacification of Ghent"; first of a series of treaties which maintained an uneasy peace until the next summer. De Requescens dies, replaced by Don Juan of Austria.

1577 Hostilities having broken out again, the North is victorious and William of Orange enters Brussels (September 23). Calvinist governments are established in most of the southern cities. Calvinism was to remain politically dominant until 1584-85.

1578 Don Juan is replaced by his assistant, Alessandro Farnese, son of Margaret of Austria. Farnese begins to regroup the Catholic forces in the Union or Arras (1579).

1585 (August 17): The capitulation of Antwerp to the Spanish completes the subjugation of Flanders. Catholicism is restored in the South, the North remaining independent. Farnese is prevented from pushing farther north by Philip's plans to invade England. The independence of the northern provinces is recognized by a truce in 1609 and by the Treaty of Westphalia in 1648.

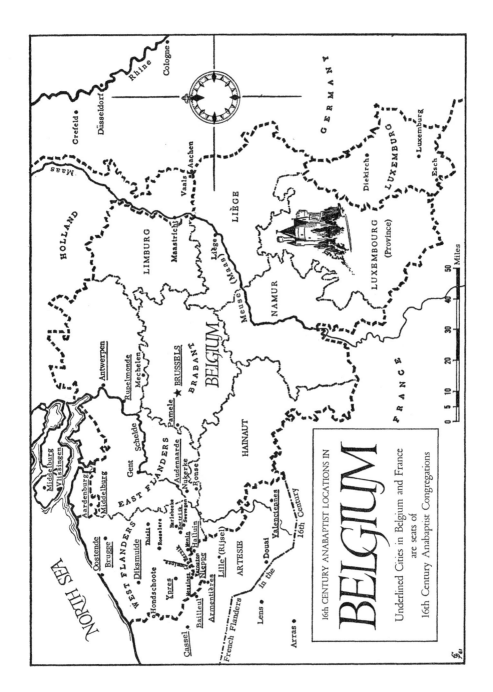

16th CENTURY ANABAPTIST LOCATIONS IN

BELGIUM

Underlined Cities in Belgium and France
are seats of
16th Century Anabaptist Congregations

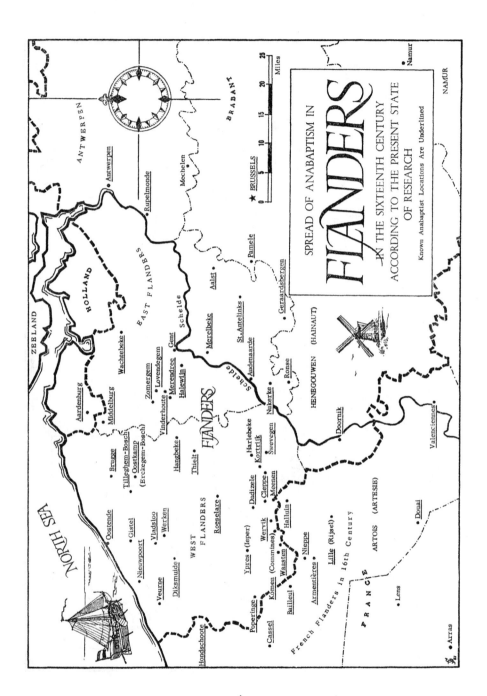

SPREAD OF ANABAPTISM IN

FLANDERS

IN THE SIXTEENTH CENTURY
ACCORDING TO THE PRESENT STATE
OF RESEARCH

Known Anabaptist Locations Are Underlined

INTRODUCTION

To seek to evoke a perfect image of the significance which Mennonitism attained in the province of Flanders during the agitated century of the Reformation seems to me to be a completely illusory enterprise. Powerful manifestations of a sharply resisting Mennonitism reveal themselves often, now in this, now in that town. Upon investigation, however, the church historian soon discovers, to his disappointment, that apart from the confirmation of a strong vitality of the brotherhood under study, he has scarcely any opportunity to penetrate into the internal life of the church. Historical research of many years has demonstrated why it will perhaps never be possible to break through this wall of mystery.

In the first place, time has wrought havoc with the archival sources. Reports of court testimony and trials—the most essential sources—reveal irreparable gaps for the sixteenth century. It is purely a stopgap method to fill the empty spots with data of the chroniclers unless they are supported by more neutral sources. In particular must we be wary in the use of quotations from the chronicles in the discussion of the history of the Mennonites in the Southern Netherlands, since the authors are either Roman Catholic or Calvinistic, and *ipso facto* can never be entirely acquitted of prejudice when they treat of Mennonitism.

A still more dangerous stumbling block is the supernatural courage with which the Mennonites answered their examining judges. The best-read as well as the least-read Mennonite under trial answered fervently the questions of his judges when he had to defend the doctrine, but was silent when he was interrogated about the organization of the group to which he belonged or about his fellow believers in other places. The most inhuman practices failed to get the tortured victim to disclose the name or the residence of his brethren who were still at liberty, and certainly not the residence of the leaders. In those cases when the one on trial did give exact indications, the persons mentioned were either already dead or out of reach at the moment of the disclosure. The rare exceptions to this general rule are the confessions of those who gave way under the menace of peril or death and the unguarded replies of children to the catch questions of trained questioners.

It is therefore not surprising that thus far Karel Vos has been the only historian to undertake the study of a Mennonite congregation in the

1

Southern Netherlands, namely, the congregation at Antwerp.[1] However, neither this fact nor the former considerations can justify the lack of interest in the study of Mennonitism in Flanders, where this religion attained such great prominence. Even if the attainment of absolute completeness is beyond reach, certainly as long as Flemish Mennonitism is so little known a very important aspect of the Reformation in the Southern Netherlands is neglected. Since the Mennonites produced nearly three quarters of the total number of Flemish martyrs and continued the struggle against the Hapsburg authority for a century, we insult logic by writing the history of the Reformation without giving a large space to Mennonitism alongside of Calvinism and Lutheranism.

For this reason, we have undertaken to write this monograph on Menno's disciples in the province of Flanders. We are aware that actually it has turned out to be no more than a "sketch" of the indefatigable activity of the Mennonites on Flemish soil.

It must be noted in advance that the historiography of the Mennonite movement will follow quite different lines, depending on whether it concerns the Northern Netherlands or the Southern Netherlands. It will not do, for example, to use for Flanders Kühler's subdivision of the history of the Mennonites of the Northern Netherlands. Kühler outlines Mennonite history in Holland as follows: The North Dutch brotherhood, from its rise until 1581, lived in a period of persecution by the state. Until 1554, however, this persecution was not of the sort to prevent the establishment of congregations, nor, after 1554, participation in great debates, which led, disappointingly enough, to numerous schisms. After 1581, the year in which the Reformed faith was elevated to the position of a state religion, the brotherhood entered a new contest with the proponents of the other Reformation churches in order to be recognized by them. This was, in effect, attained in 1672. Then the internal reconstruction was started which led to the foundation of the "Algemeene Doopsgezinde Societeit" in 1811.[2]

But this chronological division cannot be used even in part for the history of the Flemish Mennonites. In the first place, after 1640 Mennonitism in Flanders showed scarcely any signs of life. Moreover, during the entire time of its existence this faith had never received recognition as a religious movement. For the Flemish followers of Menno Simons it was "a century of struggle," although this struggle was not always equally intense. The fluctuations in the zeal of their opponents to persecute them are the only milestones in the agitated years of their existence.

---

1 K. Vos, *DtA*, p. 328.
2 Dr. W. J. Kühler, *Doopsgezinde Bijdragen*, 1917, pp. 1-8.

Originating about 1530, this movement had reached most of the centers of the country by 1550, certainly the larger ones. In this period the repression of heresy had not yet reached its height; consequently the scattered executions failed to prevent a considerable expansion. In 1550, however, came the signal for an incredibly bloody oppression. Mass arrests occurred all over the country. Many Mennonites were executed, and others were exiled for life. This storm of persecution did not decrease until 1576, when the rise of Calvinism became more and more evident. The period 1576-1586, which was (until 1584) the Golden Age for the Calvinists, eliminated the fear of death, but did not bring the recognition which the Mennonites so greatly desired.

After 1586 persecution flared up again. In this year Alessandro Farnese initiated a real hunt for the leading figures of the brotherhood, who were mercilessly condemned to death, while the ordinary members were expelled from the province. The years 1586-1640 were the period of the most obstinate resistance of the last Mennonite families who sought to be worthy of the honorable tradition of their ancestors. But it was an unequal fight. A gradual emigration to the Northern Netherlands took place, which was completed by about 1640.

Since logically our discussion has had to refer to Menno's doctrines, it will be necessary to write about the doctrines which held the chief place in the faith of the Flemish Mennonites.

The feeling of sharing a common lot, based upon and purified by incessant persecution, kept the Mennonites of the Southern Netherlands indivisible in doctrine. Here the church was always first, and individual achievements were secondary.[3] The doctrine of Menno Simons, as this Frisian elder proclaimed it at the beginning of his career, was maintained by the Flemish brotherhood to the end. Seldom did the Mennonites of the Southern Netherlands experience divergence in doctrine; those who ventured to disagree had no significant success. Nowhere were divisions completed; never was the individual to hold his own against the church.

---

3 Already in 1856 H. Q. Janssen wrote in his *Kerkhervorming te Brugge* (Rotterdam, 1856), I, p. ix, "I trust that the inclusion of the Mennonites in my history of the Reformation of the church will not meet with disapproval. They take up so large and at the same time so distinctive a place in the field of the Reformation that only narrow-mindedness can overlook them; and this disregard can only mean a great loss for historical scholarship." Gustav Bossert also criticized the lack of interest in the history of the Mennonites. What he declared in 1930 concerning the Mennonites of Württemberg can be applied just as well to the historiography of Flemish Mennonitism: "The Mennonites have been stepchildren not only of the Reformation, but also of research. Our knowledge of their world of ideas was poor, our acquaintance with the Mennonite congregations and the spread of the movement was defective, in fact almost a matter of chance. Consequently the judgments as to their significance as well as the content of their faith were uncertain and superficial, not far removed from prejudice" (*Quellen zur Geschichte der Wiedertäufer*, I, p. vo).

The actual basis of the Mennonite faith is the rejection of the sacraments. What distinguishes the Mennonites theologically from the other Reformation groups is their conception of baptism and the Lord's Supper. These doctrines were thoroughly explained by Menno Simons in his *Foundation (Fundament des Christelycken leers,* 1539). For him and thus also for his Flemish followers baptism was only a sign. First the inner battle with the devil had to be won and full surrender to God achieved; only then could baptism be considered. The administering of baptism was thus in fact the crown for the victory gained over the sinful world. Adult baptism, fundamental to the Mennonite faith, counts only as an external sign and therefore dare not in any respect have sacramental character.

Reception into the brotherhood demanded of the convert an exemplary life, a thorough knowledge of the doctrines, and a total surrender to God. When he expressed the wish to be considered for baptism, he knew that he would be subjected to a thorough examination of his faith in the presence of the bishop (the minister who had the authority to baptize) at his next visit, and he would not be surprised if his first request was fruitless.

It is worthy of note that the Mennonites did not make it easy to join their group, in spite of the severe persecutions and the infrequent visits to the Flemish area by those who were authorized to baptize. A few typical cases will suffice to illustrate this aspect of Mennonitism.

In 1550 a Mennonite youth (whose name is unknown) gave the following answer to the question asked him by the examining magistrates as to why he was not yet baptized: "Sir, when the minister questioned me about the faith, he discovered that I was still young in mind, and so he ordered me to search the Scriptures further. But I then wanted it to occur at once. Then he asked me if I knew that the world would put to death and burn such people. I said, 'I know.' Then he said unto me, 'So I asked you to have patience in this until I come back another time.' "[4] Dierick Lambrechts, also not baptized, gave the still pithier answer (August 22, 1562) "that one cannot receive baptism, since we consider that one has to reform his life beforehand."[5] The constables were still more astonished by Pieter Aelbrechts' answer in 1568 when they asked him if he would still take rebaptism if he were freed. Unreservedly the Ghent martyr declared, "Yes, I would, if I were qualified for it."[6]

It is impossible to delimit more closely the length of the period of

---

4 Van Braght, *Mirror*, II, pp. 94 f.
5 Ghent City, *Crime*, 1561-63, fol. 283.
6 Van Braght, *Mirror*, II, p. 369.

preparation for baptism. It varied for every candidate. One must also consider that there were among the brethren many who did not even possess the elementary ability to read and write. It is difficult to imagine the effort applied by these laborers to the task of familiarizing themselves with such a high world view. That their efforts were successful has been proved abundantly by the records of the examinations of those who were tortured.[7] It was not unusual for a common laborer to hold his own in the defense of the doctrine. This presupposes unquestionably a considerable intellectual maturity. Since the high demands which the bishop and the congregation made of the candidate-convert must have meant, besides a thorough purification of life, also a raising of the intellectual level in a certain sense, it is no wonder that some of the candidates for adult baptism had to wait several years. A few typical cases may serve to illustrate this.

François van der Leyen, burned at the stake at Ghent, April 28, 1558, during the trial expressed his regret that although he had faithfully attended the meetings for three years he had never been able to get so far as to deserve consideration for baptism.[8] Baerbele Pieters had to wait three years before she was received as a sister in the congregation.[9] Jossyne Swynts had to wait even longer. She had never missed the Mennonite meetings and she had endeavored to make the doctrine of Menno Simons her own. She had pressed several times to take her place as a real member of the brotherhood, but she had to wait no less than seven years before she could be baptized.[10]

The matter of baptism was naturally always the first point to be discussed in the examination of the arrested Mennonites. Nearly all the accused used the same wording in their defense, approximately as follows:

(1) The infant baptism of the Roman Catholic Church is useless and worthless;

(2) One can be baptized only when one believes and has understanding;

(3) One does not acquire salvation by baptism; it is only the sign of obedience and of a good conscience;

(4) Little children who die without baptism are nevertheless saved.[11]

Few particulars are known about the form of the ceremony of bap-

---

7 Friar Cornelis (an opponent of the Mennonites at Bruges) considered it the work of the devil that the Mennonites who could formerly not distinguish an *a* from a *b*, at their baptism suddenly knew how to read and to write. (Kühler, *loc. cit.*, p. 292.)

8 Ghent City, *Crime*, 1555-1561, fol. 58vo.

9 *Ibid.*, 1574-78, fol. 136-137.

10 Ghent City, *KR*, 1585-1605, fol. 172vo-173.

11 Ghent City, *Crime*, 1555-61, fol. 193vo.

tism itself, although it is rather generally assumed that it was done by sprinkling. The details of the practice in the South were a total mystery to us, and we had assumed without documentary confirmation that it was done here just as in the North; the discovery of the record of the trial of Godevaert Jasperssoone, who knew Flanders well, has given some clarification. He described the ceremony as follows: "One takes a dish with water, into which the minister puts his hand and then drops water upon the head of the recipient in the name of the Father, of the Son, and of the Holy Ghost upon the basis of the faith that he, the recipient, has in this baptism."[12]

Less in detail, but probably in agreement with the declaration of Jasperssoone, is the assertion of the twelve-year-old son of Jan van der Veste. The boy innocently informed the inquisitors that he had once heard his father say that his older brother and his sister were not baptized, "neither in the church nor in a brook."[13]

As regards the meaning which has been attached to the institution of the Lord's Supper, all Mennonites gave a clear testimony. All sacramental character is denied to the Supper. "It is a sign in the first place of the love of God in Christ, consequently of the unity of the believers, finally of their spiritual fellowship with the body of Christ and His death."[14] The Flemish Mennonites used sharp language to deny to the Supper all sacramental meaning. They all asserted: "That Christ is not verily in flesh and blood in the holy sacrament of the altar or consecrated host in the mass, but that this is an idol and the mass an abomination or a disgusting thing before God and that one commits idolatry when one listens to the mass or adores the sacrament of the altar."[15] To the question: "About the sacraments of the priests, do you not believe that flesh and blood is there and that it is God?" Hans Buefkin answered rather rudely: "No, sirs, I do not believe this. What! should that be flesh and blood and God? Cover this table with them, I will blow them away so that they fly about. Gods are not thus. One cannot handle God nor eat Him bodily."[16]

Adult baptism and the conception of the Supper brought the final rupture both with the Catholics and with the other Reformation groups. The other points of the Mennonite faith, however characteristic they were of the faith, only deepened the existing rupture. For the sake of

12 Brussels Royal, *EA*, No. 509, fol. 125vo.

13 Bruges City, *Bouc van den Steene*, 1558-59, fol. 89.

14 W. J. Kühler, *Geschiedenis der Nederlandsche Doopsgezinden in de zestiende eeuw* (Haarlem, 1932), p. 235.

15 Ghent City, *Crime*, 1561-63, fol. 29.

16 Van Braght, *op. cit.*, II, pp. 94 f.

completeness and clearness, however, we give a brief review of the other articles of faith.

In the course of the sixteenth century much debate in Mennonite doctrinal thinking was occasioned by the discussions about the nature of Christ. The Mennonites found it impossible to conceive that Christ bore in Himself anything of the purely human sinful nature, since His death on the cross could then not have blotted out the sins of the world. Upon this basis the Mennonites did not admit that Jesus could have received His flesh from Mary.[17] The Flemish Mennonites, in this point faithful to the guidance of their teacher Menno Simons, restricted themselves to this general view and except for some rare exceptions refrained from going on into theological fine points on this subject. Our investigation in the archives of Brussels, Antwerp, Bruges, Ghent, and Courtrai has always led to the conclusion that the followers of Menno in the Southern Netherlands in general defended against their opponents the concept that Christ was born "out of" the Virgin Mary, who remained a virgin, but not "of" Mary. This means that Christ did not receive His human nature and being from the mere body of the Virgin Mary, but that He descended from above by the power of the Holy Spirit into the Virgin,[18] as the Scriptures assert.

What Vos has reported about the doctrinal deviations bears out our conviction that they may all, however few in number, be considered sterile outgrowths.[19] Thus, the Flemish Mennonites scarcely went beyond

17 Melchior Hofmann, following in this point the spokesmen of the *devotio moderna,* described His conception in the following metaphor: "As the heavenly dew falls into the shell of a mussel and changes there into a pearl without taking over anything from the shell, so the Holy Ghost, the Word of God, fell into Mary's womb and there of itself became the spiritual pearl Jesus Christ" (*B.R.N.,* I, p. 311).

18 Brussels Royal, *EA,* No. 509, fol. 124vo-125.

19 This is what the church historian Vos reports on this subject *(DtA,* pp. 319 f.): "Regarding the liberal tendencies: the unitarian ideas of Adam Pastor, formerly a co-worker of Menno who had been excommunicated at the conference of Goch by Menno and Dirk Philips, were shared by some persons. The report of the trial of Herman van Vlekwijk, which can be found among others in van Braght and which is derived from the sermons of Friar Cornelis, indicates that this martyr was a unitarian. It is true that nothing of this can be found in the trial record, a copy of which is found in the archives at Amsterdam, but this record is certainly not complete. The well-informed Hans Alenson is the decisive authority in this matter in my opinion; he reports that Herman was a follower of Adam Pastor. It is also evident that not all Flemish Mennonites embraced the teaching of the incarnation of Christ as taken over by Menno from Hofmann. At any rate, the same Alenson claimed to possess a letter of the well-known martyr Hans Bret, the friend of Hans de Ries, which letter proves that Bret had other ideas concerning this doctrine and that he had often disputed this question with his coprisoner Jan de Vlascoper. The Flemish martyr Jacques d'Auchy, who was executed in Leeuwarden, likewise held a different attitude on the incarnation. Also Jacob van der Wege, who was burned in 1573 at Ghent, professed something different about this from what was taught by Menno."

the orthodoxy of their teacher in their conception of the Trinity. Moreover, it is noteworthy that this article of faith did not interest them very much. When questioned about it, they answered in generalities.

Still less clearly did the Flemish Mennonites develop their conception of the resurrection of the dead at the return of Jesus Christ on earth. They believed that neither purgatory nor heaven is the dwelling place for the souls of the departed; they go somewhere to await the redeeming hour of the Last Judgment. In the presence of the inquisitors they emphatically insisted that not a single saint, not even Mary, is staying in heaven, and she, like ordinary mortals, has to await the return of the Saviour. Prayers, masses, good works—nothing could change this divine decision. The fact that they considered confession, adoration of saints, fasting, and the authority of the pope not to be in accord with the requirements of the Bible certainly needs no further demonstration.

The refusal to swear oaths, the retention of nonresistance, and the use of the ban (excommunication) are also considered typical Mennonite practices.

There was agreement among all Mennonites about the swearing of the oath, testifying "that it is not allowed to swear or to take the oath if one has been compelled by the court to give witness to the truth." Since civil and political life necessitated the swearing of the oath, the Mennonites were in constant danger. In their insistence on living according to the spirit of the Gospel at any price they inevitably walked into the trap at their first examination: their refusal to take the oath immediately betrayed their belief and was practically equivalent to signing their death sentence. In this way, as will be seen later, many a Mennonite fell into the hands of the magistrates.

The Flemish followers of Menno seldom expressed themselves about the principle of nonresistance, a principle which did not achieve full recognition until the second half of the sixteenth century. It has been proved, indeed, that the brotherhood remained entirely neutral—it was, moreover, a voluntary neutrality—toward any manifestation of worldly power or use of weapons.[20] Incidentally, it can be stressed that, in contrast to the use of force at the Calvinistic hedge-sermon meetings, the Mennonite meetings were held without the aid of armed fellow believers. After the restoration of Spanish absolutism, which heralded the triumphant return of Catholicism, there were in Ghent and Bruges[21] several

---

[20] For a detailed statement on this we refer the reader to our main discussion, especially to the treatment of the attitude of the Mennonites during the Iconoclasm.

[21] E. J. Strubbe, *Het verval van het Protestantisme te Brugge na 1584 (Annales de la Société d-Emulation de Bruges*, 1924), p. 18, note 5. See also Ghent City, *Crime.* 1581-94. fol. 52 f.

instances of Mennonites refusing to serve in the civic guard. They had succeeded for a considerable time in avoiding this difficulty by hiring non-Mennonite civilians to take their places in the guard.

Except for the doctrines of the incarnation and of the Trinity, the matters of faith discussed up to this point did not cause any serious disputes. This cannot be claimed, at least for the Northern Netherlands, in respect to the question of the ban.

With great care the Mennonites sought to establish and maintain the church without "spot or wrinkle."[22] Immediately, however, the question arose as to who would be charged with discipline—the congregation or the elders (leaders of the general brotherhood). The Northern and the Southern Netherlands each solved this problem in its own distinctive way. The brotherhood of the Northern Netherlands was soon divided under the influence of the individualism of the elders desirous of leadership; this mania for division continued in fact far into the seventeenth century. The greater freedom of movement with which the Mennonites there could spread their faith was certainly not without effect. Debates could be planned unhindered, with the consequent regrettable train of divisions, a fertile subject for many pamphleteers.

The South, however, where the repression was maintained with the exception of some short periods of peace, saw the Mennonites rallying anxiously around the church and expecting from it the greatest blessing. The brethren were often thrown on their own resources, since they were frequently deprived of their leaders and, after the travels of Leenaert Bouwens (1554-56, 1557-61, 1563-65), were only rarely visited by ministers from the Northern Netherlands. Consequently it was natural that the church assume the authority to remove undesirable elements. In any case, united deliberation about certain cases necessarily diminished in actual practice the chances for inconsiderate decrees of excommunication. The Flemish Mennonites were in this respect faithful to the directives given by Menno in his Loving Admonition (Lieffelijcke Vermaninge), which was published as early as 1541. Only when the guilty brother persisted in his wickedness did the congregation have to interfere; up to that point no opportunity to restore the erring to the right path was neglected. This spirit, which was dissipated in the North under the pressure of particularistic animosities, persisted undiminished in the South.

---

22 The fundamentals of the "blameless church which is without spot or wrinkle" can be summarized as follows according to the spirit of Menno Simons (K. Vos, Menno Simons, p. 195): (1) Holding fast to the unadulterated teaching and the acceptance of the ministers ordained by God; (2) Scriptural observance of the sacraments; (3) brotherly love; (4) keeping the commandments of God; (5) bearing suffering and persecution for Christ's sake; (6) open confession of God and Christ.

The first testimony about this dates from 1551. Hans van Overdam indicated very clearly the road they had to take. "You must," he declared, "go to them [the erring ones] and rebuke them, and if they do not want to hear this you must bring them before the church and rebuke them in public. If they do not hearken then, put them out of church and treat them as Gentiles and public sinners." Admonition from man to man, handling the case within the church and only then expulsion—this was the way in which the weapon of excommunication was used in the South. They considered as "a wrinkle or spot" those who committed theft, lying (this was considered as a serious delinquency), adultery, or other acts contrary to the general Christian teaching.

Jacques de Rore, one of the most influential leaders of the second half of the sixteenth century, expressed himself similarly in his extant correspondence. In one of his letters, addressed to the Mennonite Pauwels van Meenen, who had inquired of him concerning the question of shunning, he touched a thorny aspect of congregational life. De Rore gave plainly his judgment about the attitude to be taken toward fellow believers who maintained contact with the erring ones. Even here he urged caution and asked them not to consider the delinquent from the beginning as an enemy, "but to admonish him as a brother, for the admonition serves to improvement, likewise the shunning and the excommunication serve to improvement."[23] Thus tolerance became the principal characteristic of the Mennonitism of the Southern Netherlands; yet this prudent wielding of the weapon of excommunication never degenerated into laxity.

Of Jan Dhauwere it was said in 1559 that the brethren "avoided him because he still frequented the taverns."[24] Petronelle van de Velde, who fell into the hands of the tribunal of Ghent in 1563, presents an extreme case: illegitimate children, the use of dishonest means to obtain money, a veritable mania for lying and regular lawsuits—all this was charged against her when she expressed the wish to be admitted to the circle of emigré Flemish Mennonites in London. Lowys "of Flanders" admitted her in spite of all these wrongs. Before this, the Flemish leader had brought her before the brotherhood and compelled her to confess real penitence and to promise that she would show herself worthy of the baptism she received. Her behavior was for some time blameless, for after her return to Flanders her marriage to Antheunis van Steen at

---

23 Jacob de Rore, *Lieflijcke Brieven* (edition of 1584, fol. Ji, vo). Herman de Timmerman also stood energetically in the breach for the mild application of excommunication in a well-written pamphlet. (Vos. *op. cit.*, p. 329.) Vos also treats this martyr in his *Menno Simons* (Leiden, 1914), pp. 147-49.

24 Ghent City, *Crime*, 1555-61, fol. 100vo.

Ghent was consecrated by the noted Flemish elder, Hans Busschaert, called the Weaver. When, however, a short time thereafter she again gave evidence of yielding to worldly temptations, the injured congregation acted boldly: after deliberation it excommunicated her and declared her marriage void.[25]

The affair of Fierin Grysperre provides a vivid testimony of the authority vested in the congregation in respect to the pronouncing of excommunication. This time it was not a matter of one having abandoned himself to worldly practices. On the contrary, Grysperre was one of the ministers of the Ghent congregation, who after personal study had come to conclusions which were not completely in accord with Menno's teaching. Approached immediately about this matter, he obstinately maintained his point of view. Evidently he was then summoned before a wider circle, but without success. On the ground that the accused would not submit, he was expelled from the brotherhood. Fierin Grysperre thereupon appealed to the full congregation. He expressed himself as follows: "Because he was not excommunicated by *all* the brethren and sisters of the congregation, he gave them to understand that he would prove that he had to be heard before *all* the brethren and sisters, since he was only excommunicated by *some* of them and not in the presence of *all* of the brethren."[26] The final decision, according to this testimony of 1582, belonged most positively to the congregation.

In the light of this, the signficance of the Mennonite conference which was held at Antwerp in August, 1567, can better be grasped. This meeting (where not only Mennonites of Antwerp were present) had been arranged especially to consider which fellow believers could no longer be tolerated because of persistence in a licentious life.[27]

The weapon of excommunication, exercised by the whole brotherhood, can frequently, for the South, not be considered an evil. The Flemish Mennonites always preferred tolerance without laxity, and expelled only hardened "sinners."

For these reasons we cannot follow Kühler in concluding, on the basis of the attitude of Hans de Ries and Charles de Nielles, that the Southern Netherlands followed the North on the road of divisions. Both of the testimonies quoted come from Antwerp Mennonite circles. Apart from the fact that the metropolis was influenced more by spokesmen from

25 *Ibid.*, 1563-65, fol. 47-55, 172, 284-285.

26 *Ibid.*, 1581-83, fol. 172.

27 At the same meeting they discussed the "candidate brethren," whose cases were investigated carefully, since they wanted above all other things to keep the level of the spiritual life of the brotherhood qualitatively high. (Marcus van Vaernewijck, *Van die beroerlicke tijden*, 5vo. (Ghent, 1872-1881) II., pp. 341 f.)

the Northern Netherlands, who could move about there more freely than elsewhere because of the greater density of population, it is at least rash to equate the spiritual life in the Antwerp congregation with that of the whole Flemish brotherhood, which had to contend with totally different conditions.

"Endeavor always to build up one another"—these were the parting words of Jacques de Rore to the leaders of Flemish Mennonitism.[28] Those who are familiar with the history of the Mennonites in the province can see in these words the answer that directed all followers of Menno Simons to unite in order to sustain for a century the unequal struggle with the confederated powers of church and state in the country of Flanders, a land deprived of its liberty of thought.

We have no other purpose than to light up this heroic struggle in order better to understand the Flemish Reformation.

A. L. E. Verheyden

---

28 Jacob de Rore, *Lieflijcke Brieven,* fol. Q.vj.vo.

I. RISE OF THE
FLEMISH BROTHERHOODS: 1530-1550

The religious emancipation of the sixteenth century in Flanders was not a sudden outburst but only the final phase of a consistent development from roots far in the past. The last decades of the fourteenth century had already been powerfully influenced by an impulse seeking real and deep religious experience, free of all dogmatic prejudice, an impulse which could no longer be suppressed.[1]

The activity of the Brethren of the Common Life in bringing the Bible to the people in the vernacular, which released the individual from conformist thinking and enabled him to express his religious views freely, penetrated into the broadest areas of contemporary Flemish society.

Of course the "modern devotion" movement, being a creation of the Middle Ages, was still attached to the prestige of the decadent Catholic Church; nevertheless the masses of the people were aroused from their ancient religious rigidity by the creative preaching and the revivalistic writing of Geert de Groote's followers.

This nonecclesiastical revival defied the spirit of the time and counted ever more followers in the fifteenth and especially in the sixteenth century, while the clerical dignitaries in the period were straying further and further from their religious calling. The Catholic priests indeed presented a tragic scene of unprecedented lawlessness, and boldly committed the gravest immoralities, thus broadening the gap between them and the hungering seekers for sincere peace of soul.

Claes de Praet, a Mennonite martyr of 1556, summarized the decadence among the clergy in this satirical tirade: "You preach to the people not to get drunk, but you yourselves walk the streets as drunk as swine. You preach to the people not to be stingy, but where can more avarice be found than among priests and monks? You preach to the people not to be idle, but where can more idleness be found than with you? You'd

---

1 Paul Frédéricq, *Corpus documentorum inquisitionis haereticae pravitatis Neerlandicae* (Ghent and The Hague, 1879-1906), I, pp. 299, 361, 363 f., 397, 444, 446, 458, 500 f.; II, pp. 97, 99, 101 f., 106, 111 f., 114, 226, 267; III, pp. 3, 13 f. 19, 76-78, 141-43.

go from door to door with a sack or a basket as beggars rather than work. That's what we see."[2]

Until now the church had succeeded in saving its prestige either by adopting any religious revival or by crushing it in its very beginning as a dangerous heresy, but now it succumbed, undermined by unscrupulous representatives.

The Reformation idea, however, expressed itself in different ways. In this age of religious individualism the reaction against the inadequate clergy and the petrifying codes of dogma could not but lead away from the church. The three waves of reform which reached the Netherlands in the course of the sixteenth century did not show, in their attitude toward Catholicism, the great differentiation that might have been expected from the dogmatic differences.

In their attempt to restore real significance to religion as a living factor in folk consciousness Martin Luther and John Calvin, each in his own way, made fundamental changes in the traditional doctrines, but essentially both replaced the Catholic Church and its dogma by their churches and their dogma. Thus the history of Lutheranism and of Calvinism is that of two distinct church groupings, which never deviated from the original dogmatic concepts of their respective founders.

Both elements—church and dogma—lose for a great part their authoritative character among the Anabaptists, to whom the ideas of the elders—these are the leaders of the movement—are only directives in the realization of their religious ideal, which is a consistent *imitatio Christi*. In contrast with the tempered individualisms of Lutherans and Calvinists, they became ardent advocates of a personal experience of God's Word, and such a conception caused no little difference of opinion.

From the beginning Anabaptism had two aspects: while numerous zealots were swept away by the hope of having the whole world at their feet before long and, as the elect, of escaping the imminent destruction of the heathen (i.e., all non-Anabaptists!), the others—originally a minority—were dedicated to an ideal which renounced the world and shunned violence, and devoted their best efforts to the building of a peaceful brotherhood, which was to include all "who believe in Christ's name."

The former group won a quick victory over the pacifist-minded group in the Northern Netherlands; the call to action issued by Jan van Leiden, Jan Matthijs van Haarlem, and others found such a good response that many magistrates looked with fear at the growth of the revolutionary idea within their respective jurisdictions. It did not, how-

2 *B.R.N.*, II, pp. 251 f.

ever, progress beyond this promising start: Münster (which was to become the New Jerusalem!) surrendered to the bishop's armies, the movement of the Adamites at Amsterdam was merely a brief hysterical show, and the assault on the Oldeklooster near Bolsward was a tragic fiasco.

This series of failures inevitably had serious consequences. First of all, it furnished the secular authorities with an easy legal justification for their draconic repressive measures against the peaceful Anabaptists. Though fundamentally absolutely different, the peaceful Anabaptists were always equated with the revolutionary Anabaptists of the beginning and consequently no penalty was too severe for them. (For anyone familiar with the martyrology of the Southern Netherlands, it is no secret that the worst death penalties, such as burning at the stake or burial alive, were inflicted on the Mennonites.)

The actual spiritual life of the brotherhood also underwent decisive change. The peaceful brethren, who had previously had to be silent, now left their minority position and assumed the leadership. Flemish Anabaptism did not, however, suffer so violently under the storm that raged over the Northern Netherlands brotherhood.

About 1530 Melchiorite teachings had penetrated into the cities of Bruges[3] and Ghent,[4] and then spread rapidly in the Southern Flemish cities and villages. The first indications are too vague to determine with certainty from what area the new faith first came to Flanders. The first acquaintance with Hofmann's doctrines was probably made directly under German influence. First of all, the German merchants[5] and also the Flemish businessmen[6] did their part, just as they had for Lutheranism

---

3 Verheyden, *Bruges*, p. 14.

4 B. de Jonghe, the chronicler of Ghent, writes: "Ever since 1530 there were some people around and about Ghent infected with the heresies of the Anabaptists" (de Jonghe, *Ghent*, I, p. 2).

The historian V. Fris exaggerates when he states in his *Histoire de Gand* (Ghent, 1930), p. 187: "Already before 1534 the teleobaptists were swarming." Fris has stretched de Jonghe's statement too far. See Verheyden, *DtG*, pp. 99 ff.

5 Dieric van Eeno, arrested at Bruges, declared without hesitation (though his declaration was made after 1540, it is still typical of the entire period): "I talked with a German. It is much better in Germany than here; the people over there are much more sincere; they do not go to civil court like here; they live in a more brotherly way; whoever is well-to-do shares with the others. If it were not for my children, I'd have gone there long ago" (Bruges City, *Informatiën*, 1542-47, fol. 115).

6 In early 1535 the case of Cornelis de Clerc was investigated at Bruges. Shortly before he had returned from Lübeck and had told his fellow citizens many things about his visit there. He said among other things, "They baptized three there sooner than one here, and [he] wonders whether water makes that much difference" (Bruges City, *Informatie bouc, 1532-1538,* fol. 79-80vo). This testimony does not belong chronologically in the birth years of Anabaptism; yet it indicates the important role of Flemish merchants in the propagation of the new views. Slowly the government's distrust of certain Eastern countries grew. Some years later all

a decade before, to give the new faith the necessary publicity on Flemish soil. Furthermore, it should be noted that after the ruthless condemnation of Anabaptism by the Diet of Spires in 1529 many Anabaptists fled to the Meuse provinces[7] and thus it is not at all impossible that many a refugee may have had the impulse to hide in the protective shadow of the great Flemish industrial and commercial cities.

It is quite a different problem to explain the actual organized propagation of the new teachings. It appears that the northern neighbors with their closely related language were better able to bring the new doctrines even to the smallest villages. About 1532 some merchants from Zeeland stopped to visit Flanders, ostensibly for business reasons, but really, under the pretext of their trade, to help the new ideas take root in the broad and receptive Flemish field. It was this close connection with the Anabaptist movement of the Northern Netherlands which exposed the South, during the period of crisis, to the dangers of revolutionary degeneration which we have already mentioned.

W. J. Kühler asserts, in his excellent work on Dutch Anabaptism in the sixteenth century, that the Southern Netherlands did not participate in this conflict; personally I am inclined toward a different view. I believe that the temptation to resort to violent methods like those of the Northern Netherlands brethren[8] also existed in some Flemish Anabaptist circles, but was not responded to with the same enthusiasm.

---

contact with the county of Cleve was prohibited because of the strong Anabaptist movement there. (Edict of the Bruges Council, March 28, 1545; Bruges City, *Hallegeboden*, 1543-53, fol. 160vo-161vo.) A noteworthy edict of June 15, 1542, at Antwerp proclaimed: "Anabaptists, rebaptizers, and other evil-minded fellows are reported lying in wait along the Meuse with the intent of attacking some of the cities of His Imperial Majesty; whoever has heard anything about this shall report it" (Génard, *AA*, I, p. 215).

7 P. Frédéricq, *Travaux pratiques, Sur le fait d'hérésie au Pays de Liége* (Ghent, 1883), pp. 39 f. The revolt of the Anabaptist "Rivageois" in July, 1531, is typical in this context. A huge crowd, streaming from the villages along the Meuse, massed together before the gates of the prince-episcopal city of Liége. In vain they tried to enter the city. But they had a discussion with some Liége authorities; the Anabaptists demanded, among other things, the release of Jehan Halbert, the reduction of bread prices, and the confiscation of the stocks of grain in the monasteries. The prince-bishop did not yield and had the leaders of the revolt arrested; some were tortured or beheaded and others were exiled. See Jean Meyhoffer, *Le martyrologe protestant* (Nessonvaux, 1907), p. 169; Charles Rahlenbeck, *L'Eglise de Liége* (Brussels, 1864), pp. 45 f., 55-59; Fer. J. Henaux, *Histoire du Pays de Liége* (Liége, 1872-74), II, pp. 251-56; Guillaume de Meeff, *La mutinerie des Rivageois* (Liége, 1835); Comte de Becdelievre, *Biographie liégeoise* (Liége, 1836-37), I, pp. 216 f.

8 B. Stroman, "Wederdoopers," in *Vrije Bladen*, Vol. IX, No. 12. An appeal addressed to all Anabaptists read: "All believing companions in Christ, grace and peace be unto you from God through His Son Jesus Christ, Amen. Dear brethren and sisters, arrange to meet half a mile outside Hasselt around Berch Cloister, on March 24, about noon; be careful in every respect; you should not be there before this date, nor later; after this time we shall wait for no one; let no one fail to come; if anyone stays back, I am innocent of his blood" (*op. cit.*, p. 6).

In the spring of 1534 Jan van Geelen, an Anabaptist agitator, appeared at Antwerp to establish a circle of the "elect." However little success he may have had, his first followers here—Geert de Smid, Jostijn de Wever, Jacop de Barbier, Peter Jacops, Thies de Droogscheerder, Leentgen, Nieskens, Jan van Luik, Lieven de Juwelier, Jan Smid, and Tonnys—very probably made every attempt to spread the Anabaptist teachings outside the metropolis after the departure of their leader.[9] Likewise it is not impossible that Leenaerdt de Boeckbinder of Antwerp baptized in the South as Jan Matthijs' emissary, even though his activity is reported only in Zierikzee.[10]

Anabaptist views also reached the Flemish groups in a more direct way by means of the travels of Cornelis van Valconisse[11] and Pieter van Gelder.[12]

Cornelis was a former priest from the abbey at Hulst, who in the spring 1534 was arrested in Vilvoorde because of Anabaptist preaching. Subjected to examination on the rack, he did not hesitate to confess his contact with outstanding revolutionary Anabaptists from the North. He had spoken repeatedly with Jan van Leiden, who time and again tried to sweep him into his blind fanaticism, pointing out to him the hundreds of disciples who wandered throughout the country calling everyone to join the fellowship of the elect, who would be assured of salvation on the imminent Day of Judgment. During these conversations Cornelis became acquainted with the exclusive spirit of the revolutionary leaders and their promise of a new society with community of goods. Strongly influenced by these radical teachings, the ex-priest, upon his

Furthermore, see the remarkable letter of the Düsseldorf authorities reporting the doctrines carried by the Münsterite emissaries (among them Jan van Geelen), partly published in Verheyden, *Bruges*, p. 15.

9 Vos, *DtA*, p. 317. W. J. Kühler, *Geschiedenis der Nederlandsche Doopsgezinden . . . ,* p. 64. No trace can be found of any of the other eleven emissaries of Jan Matthysz in Flanders. According to the Catholic author "V. P." in his *Successio Anabaptistica* (1603), they were Bartel Boeckbinder, Dirck Cuper, Gerit Boeckbinder, Jacop van Campen, Peter Scheymaker, David van Hoorn, Lenaerdt Boeckbinder, Cornelis uwt den Briel, Claes van Alkmaer, Meynaerdt van Delft, and Peter Houtsager (concerning their activities see *Doopsgezinde Bijdragen*, 1917, p. 98). (Translator's note: All of the surnames here are professional or geographical names. Since, however, the use of fixed hereditary surnames was not generally practiced in the sixteenth and seventeenth centuries, and the professional or geographical epithets served almost as surnames, we shall, at the request of Dr. Verheyden, generally leave them untranslated.)

10 *Doopsgezinde Bijdragen*, 1917, p. 104. Vos, *op. cit.*, p. 318.

11 Brussels Royal, *Office fiscal du Brabant*, carton 1, 194.

12 "Register of the suits which the provosts and aldermen of the city of Courtrai have pending before the Council of Flanders about Easter 1534" *(Perkamijnen privilegieboeck, I,* fol. 103). This lawsuit also was the cause of a conflict between the Courtrai Council and the Bishop of Tournai, which was decided in Courtrai's favor. (Ch. Mussely, *Inventaire des archives de la ville de Courtrai* [Courtrai, 1921], II, pp. 68 f.)

return to the South, could not help spreading the new ideas; thus he was until the moment of his arrest an involuntary (so he pictured it at his trial in Vilvoorde) propagandist of the Anabaptist teachings. The date of his arrest (the spring of 1534) precludes his having said anything about the course of the Münster tragedy.

Another former clergyman, Pieter van Gelder, took this task upon himself after having participated in the experiences in Westphalia for a time. According to his declaration to the magistracy of Courtrai in September, 1535, he visited several coast cities and Southern Flemish towns after his return from Münster, mingling with the Anabaptists. There he often showed some strange coins, one of pure gold, the others of ordinary brass, both sides of which were covered by a cross encircled by certain letters; on one side I.P.E.O.C. and on the other Q.C.E.B.Q. F.S.E.[13] The former priest, still full of his visit to Münster, was only too eager to translate these characters to his audience: "Ite predicate evangelium omni creaturae; que crediderit enim baptisatus que fuerit salvus erit." (Go and preach the Gospel to every creature; he who believes and is baptized will be saved.) During his trial Peter van Gelder confessed that he was an Anabaptist.

It is thus certain that these and other propagandists actually spread the revolutionary theories of the Amsterdam and Westphalian groups among Flemish Anabaptists. According to Lalaing, Count of Hoogstrate, Flemings are supposed to have participated in the tragic voyage of the Anabaptist volunteers who were going to liberate Münster.[14] Yet, generally speaking, the radical movement did not have the same destructive results here as in the North.

Cornelis Pieterszoon Hooft, a member of the Amsterdam government, said in 1611 concerning the conditions among the Northern Netherlands Anabaptists, "They would have had an easier road if they

13 P. Catrou, *Histoire des Anabaptistes* (Amsterdam, 1699), p. 83, reproduces sketches of three Münster coins. One bears on its face the inscription, "Johan van Leiden, King of the Anabaptists, Münster" (with image), and on the reverse side, "God's might is my strength, Anno MDXXXVI." (Translator's note: The date MDXXXVI is distinctly visible on the coin; it is presumably an engraver's error for MDXXXIV. Other coins in the collection bear the Arabic figures "1534." In the Paris edition of Catrou's work [1706] this sketch is on p. 419; in Lambertus Hortensius' *Verhaal van de Oproeren der Wederdoopers* . . . [Amsterdam, 1699] it faces p. 159. A. Wevers Jr. has given a careful description and photographic reproduction in his *Munten en penningen der Münstersche Wederdoopers* . . . [Enschede, 1933].)

14 Lalaing reports this trip as follows in a communication to Charles (April 2, 1534): "Through the Council here I have learned, by a letter from the magistrates of your city of Campen, that as many as twenty-seven boats have harbored in the river and sea near Campen, full of men, women, and girls, three thousand in number, coming not only from Holland, but also from Brabant, Flanders, Zeeland, and Friesland, intending to cross over from there to Münster" (Brussels Royal, *ms. divers*, no. 794 A, fol. 167).

had reduced all those distinctions to two branches, the materialists and the spiritualists."[15] In the southern brotherhood Hooft's wishes were reality; even more, here the superiority of the spiritualists over the materialists was never in doubt. The brotherhood always was true to the peaceful and spiritual principles which were the basis of the first congregation. Not only did the appeal of Rothmann's *Van der Wrake*[16] ring very faintly in the Flemish country, but after the collapse of the Münster tragedy, the Anabaptists here rapidly rallied to the discipline of faith promoted by the Frisian Menno Simons. Already in 1536 Menno declared all use of force as absolutely unacceptable and strongly rejected the building of a church and a kingdom of God on earth by the sword.[17] When he expounded his anti-Münsterite conception, it was in extremely plain language. "I have never seen Münster, nor have I ever been in their fellowship. I trust that by the grace of God I shall never eat nor drink with such . . . unless they truly repent."[18] The same spirit filled the Flemish Mennonites. In several martyr hymns these words recur time and again, and during this century the inquisitional judges more than once heard identical statements.

In the South the "quiet" Melchiorites gratefully seized the first stable guidance which corresponded to their own aspirations, and from then on, Flemish Anabaptism followed the path of Northern Mennonitism. The others, at least the majority of them, tragically deceived in the great expectations prophesied by the Münsterite leaders, came to their senses after the example of Obbe Philips[19] and joined the ranks of the "peace-

15 Christiaan Sepp, *Geschiedkundige Nasporingen* (Leyden, 1872-73), I, p. 154.

16 Christiaan Sepp, *op. cit.,* I, pp. 55-157. This Mennonite minister of Leiden gives details concerning the often-mentioned but little-known writings of the Anabaptist Bernard Rothmann. Among the outstanding participants in the defense of Münster we find no Flemish. The best-known Anabaptists in the Westphalian episcopal city were Bernard Knipperdolling, Bernard Rothmann, Herman Bisbink, Brixius, Johan van Wyck, Jan Matthijszoon (Enoch), Jan Beukelszoon (Elias), Hendrik Roll, Hendrick Strapedius, Theodor Fabritius, Johan Lening, Jehan Schröder, Kloprijs, Strahe, Bernard Mummen, Arnold Belz, Georg zum Berge and his sixteen-year-old daughter, Peter Schemaker, Jan van Geel, Hubert Rasscher, Heinrich Redecker, Herman Tilbeck, Heinrich Mohlenbecke, Schlachtschap, Vinnius, Johann van Utrecht, Dusentschur, Niland, Willem Bart, Hilla Feycken, Bernard Krechting, and Johan Died. van Batenburg. (*De Navorscher*, XIV [1912], p. 201.)

17 Cramer, *Realenzyklopädie für Protestantische Theologie*, 3d ed., XII, p. 606.

18 Menno, *Complete Writings*, p. 547.

19 B. Stroman, *Wederdoopers*, p. 23 f. Obbe Philips wrote: "For all of us were simple like children and did not suspect that we would be deceived by our own brethren, who every day were with us in the same deadly dangers." Obbe describes Melchior Hofmann's fate with this lament: "The most merciful God take pity on and be merciful to his poor soul. For it will be easily understood by every sane man how his heart felt, as the time of his prophecy passed by, and no salvation, help, nor consolation came to him; as he had to admit as false and counterfeit all that he had proclaimed so boldly from the mouths of prophets and prophetesses; and that he had been deceived by all their visions, prophecies, missions, and

ful." A few persevered for some time in their plans to change the religious and social order, but the rare aberrations never met with success; always it was evident that their following was small and the influence of their ideas weak.

Since the study of these aberrations does not fall in the framework of the subject at hand, I limit myself to the discussion of a few revolutionary outbursts.

About 1535 in Ghent, the city which with its restless industrial population seemed predestined to adopt this socially slanted confession, there developed such a revolutionary Anabaptist community under the leadership of Mahieu Waghens.[20] Spreading in the proletarian environment amidst workers yearning for economic improvement, the Anabaptist faith was very soon strongly influenced by this social struggle. We observe this interaction between religious experience and reaction against social oppression at its best in the account, *Relation des troubles de Gand sous Charles-Quint par un anonyme,* in which the author accompanied every mention of Protestants (whom he calls Lutherans, but whom we believe to be Anabaptists of the revolutionary sort) with the words: "who likewise sought only to stir them up, in order to have all things in common."[21]

The new spirit which filled those who lived apart from the Catholic Church could not have been expressed more sharply. Seen in this light the Lutherans (Anabaptists) of Ghent in this period before 1540 spoke a very clear language when, already enraged by social injustice, they took up the battle against the local clergy and the ecclesiastical abuses. As for the Anabaptist group, they objected (according to Mahieu Waghens) to the baptism of bells, picturing it as an absolutely heathen practice.

Though these threats were only of local character, yet the attitude revealed here represents more than that of the Ghent Anabaptists alone. The cross-examinations of other prisoners show that this group stood in close relation to the Southern and Eastern Flemish communities;[22]

dreams, and in his calling as the new Elijah. My heart has pity on him to this day, in such a sorrow of his soul, which certainly has been much harder to him than all persecution and tyranny, as every reasonable man can easily imagine."

20 Ghent City, *Crime,* 1538-39, fol. 3-3vo, 7-7vo, 9vo-10.

21 L. P. Gachard, *Relation des troubles de Gand sous Charles-Quint par un anonyme* (Brussels, 1840), pp. 5, 23, 35, 40, 216. "Lesquelz ne tendoient pareillement que a mectre toute commotion en iceulx, affin en faire toutes choses communes." Conditions in Ghent became very critical in September, 1539, according to the pastor of the St. Jacobs Church, Andries de Sceppere. He addressed his parishioners in that month thus: "They say that all churches, monasteries, and convents will be razed, the brethren driven out and burned within five years" (Ghent City, *Crime,* 1538-39, fol. 122vo). Concerning these riots in Ghent, see further Verheyden, *DtG,* pp. 103 f.

22 Cf. Verheyden, *DtG,* pp. 101 f. Among the places mentioned are Bruges, Poperinge,

thus here also there were brethren (this is the way these fellow believers always addressed each other, expressing their sincere attachment with the kiss upon greeting or parting) who had not yet given up the hope of achieving by action what the absolute majority of Mennonites tried to achieve by word alone—the purification of spiritual life. It is remarkable that the Ghent Anabaptists in this period received support from peddlers from Zeeland, among whom one named Lauwereyns was outstanding in his particularly active preaching in the East Flemish capital, while on the other hand Mahieu Waghens often visited Zeeland, which had been strongly influenced by Münsterite ideology.[23]

Since the movement in the Ghent group, except for its tendency to violence, still held a Biblical Anabaptist position, it can in no way be connected with the more threatening manifestations of antisocial Anabaptism like that of the Batenburgers. Jan van Batenburg—executed on April 5, 1538, at Vilvoorde—[24] had fully accepted the Münsterite ideology, and during his trial confessed having attended several meetings where the seizure of certain cities by the "elect" was discussed.[25] His antisocial and antinomian teachings survived for a long time after his execution, for traces of this Münsterite aberration can still be found in the second half of the sixteenth century. Religion was for these Batenburgers nothing but a covering for countless sensual ideas. Their only connection with the Reformation was that they fought the Catholics and that they had a certain sympathy for all non-Catholic thought. They spoke of a kingdom of God on earth, since they saw in this an opportunity, as the fellowship of the elect, to rule the world and to appropriate all earthly goods. They justified theft by the assumption that no one who did not belong to their exclusive group had any right to possessions, since all things on earth belonged to God and *ipso facto* to those who served Him best, that is, to themselves.

When at one of the Batenburger meetings a decision was passed to make an attack, the group sometimes went through a peculiar formality

---

Ypres, and Vieux-Berquin (French Flanders). Also significant for the period 1535-40 are the following accounts of executed Flemish Mennonites: In 1537 Philippus de Keurs executed at Cassel (French Flanders) (van Braght, *Mirror*, II, p. 41); on September 9, 1538, at Vucht ('s Hertogenbosch) the weaver Jan Blok from Ghent was burned (*ibid.*, II, p. 41.).

23 Considering this data, it is apparent that Pierre Tayspil was misinformed when he wrote on June 14, 1538, to the regent Maria of Hungary: "Madame, this morning the imperial attorney general and I were warned about a certain number of Lutherans and Anabaptists said to be residing one or two leagues from this city, which has no dangerous elements in its population except for those of this sect" (Alexandre Henne, *Histoire de Charles V* [Brussels, 1850-60], VI, p. 247, note 2; IX, p. 73, note 1).

24 Brussels Royal, *EA*, no. 1504.

25 *Ibid.*

before going into action. If the threatened institution was a convent, they previously attended the wedding of a daughter; if the attack was to be directed against a monastery, they appeared first at the wedding ceremony of a son.

On moral questions they held from the beginning to sensual degeneracy in a loose kind of polygamy; a man was actually allowed to have as many wives as he could support. If one of these wives gave any sign of resenting this humiliating life, she was mercilessly dragged away to a secret place by some members of the community and killed by the minister with his own hands.

This last fact proves, in addition to the denial of every moral value, the great prestige of the ministers. Their ordination was always accompanied by several solemn ceremonies; after a time of complete abstinence, all the members prayed for a long time before they cast their vote in favor of one or the other "candidate-minister." The elected minister was from that moment on not only the absolute ruler of the congregation, but also the only one to have regular contact with the highest authority, a group of eighteen men with headquarters in Antwerp.

The secrecy of their organization explains largely why these Batenburg congregations could develop their activities unpunished. To gain membership one had to survive a whole series of severe tortures to assure that in the event of arrest and torture the Batenburger would not betray his fellows. Some members arrested at Bruges in December, 1564, could not be made to confess until the police officers systematically kept them from sleeping.[26]

---

26 Kervyn de Lettenhove, *Documents relatifs à l'histoire du XVIe siècle*, I (Brussels, 1883), pp. 13-20. De Lettenhove publishes a letter from Fr. Lorenço de Villa-Vicencio to a minister of Philip II (1565) concerning the arrest at Bruges of a group of Batenburgers and the resulting revelations. In his introduction to this letter de Lettenhove expounded on the sect of the House of Love *(Huis der Liefde)*, which had its seat in the county of Cleve. Other interesting sources about the Batenburgers are the following: *B.R.N.*, Vol. V (introduction to Adam Pastor's *Underscheit tusschen Rechte en Valsche Leer)*; Alf. Journez, "Fray Lorenço" (in P. Frédéricq, *Travaux pratiques*, second fascicle, Ghent, 1884, pp. 61 f.); K. Vos, "Wanneer eindigt de 'Munstersche' beweging?" (in *Doopsgezinde Bijdragen*, 1917, p. 141, where Ghent is mentioned). From Journez' study we quote here as illustration some passages from Lorenço's letter: "They all [i.e., the Batenburgers] assemble in a country house. For three days no piece of clothing covers their bodies. After that the votes are cast and he who has the most votes is appointed minister. The name they give him is gatherer *(congregador)* or 'marrier.' This minister has authority to marry and to divorce; he gives to everyone as many wives as he can support. Until the present, those who have had the most have six; others have four; most of them have two. The wives are not allowed to address their husband except as 'Lord'; they base this on the fact that Abraham was called thus by his wife Sarah. After supper the husband chooses the wife who is to sleep with the lord; they cannot recommend nor present themselves. They recite certain verses, and she who says the last one will sleep with the lord. When any one of the wives gives signs of disgust for this kind of life

The deviations from the essentially peaceful Mennonite teachings,[27] of which the movements of Mahieu Waghens and Jan van Batenburg were the most influential in Flanders, did not, however, in any way endanger the beginning and later expansion of Menno Simons' faith. After 1540 Mennonitism flowered even more openly on Flemish ground; the major industrial cities as well as the smaller towns in the country had by then either fully organized churches or the first foundations for a later congregation.

This first general spreading of Mennonitism in Flanders was followed by a sharpening of the imperial edicts. The mandates of October 10, 1535, January 24, 1539, and December 14, 1541,[28] were especially meant to exterminate the Mennonites. No extenuating circumstances were to be considered in their trials. Charles V simply put them in the same category as the thieving wandering mercenaries and pictured them thus: "They seek for nothing but an occasion to find means to attack any town or fort, to fortify themselves and make war against all good Christians, as we experienced in the past in the city of Münster."[29]

Mark Martens, at Brussels, and Jacob van Liesvelt, at Antwerp, published this edict under the significant title, "Placcaet ende edict tegen 't concept ende voornemen der Anabaptisten ende andere quaetwillige"[30] (Mandate and Edict Against the Plot and Enterprise of the Anabaptist and Other Evil-Minded Persons). The Southern Netherlands Mennonites retained this tag of "evil-minded" until the end of the century. In 1535 Cornelis Grapheus at Antwerp had already published his *Monstrum Anabaptisticum rei Christianae pernicies*.[31] In this book the Anabaptists

---

or gives her husband any reason for dissatisfaction, he complains to the minister; she is dragged into the woods and the minister kills her. One such minister has thus put to death six or seven persons. They baptize their children, not for the remission of their sins or for the bestowing of grace, but to avoid scandal and not being able to live like other citizens. They have nurses with them who teach their children. The reason they permit several wives is the desire to see this holy company grow; they call upon the authority of the Old Testament, according to which polygamy existed among the patriarchs."

27 We mention finally two exceptional cases. In 1535 Anna Baelhuys (also called Annetgen Jansdochter) of Brussels was arrested because she had participated in the Amsterdam riot, as had also her husband. (Grete Grosheide and Abraham Hulshof, *Wederdoopers te Haarlem en te Amsterdam* [Hilversum, 1940], p. 124.) In 1551 five Anabaptists who had destroyed a crucifix and images of saints on the dike near Austruweel were executed at Antwerp. (Vos, *DtA*, p. 364.)

28 During the first wave of repression the mandates were issued on May 8, 1521, July 17, 1526, October 14, 1529, October 7, 1531, June 10, 1535, and February 17, 1535 (1536 n.st.).

29 Ch. Laurent, ed., *Ordonnances des Pays-Bas*, second series (Brussels, 1893-1922), IV, pp. 74, 104 f.

30 P. A. Tiele, *Bibliotheek van Nederlandsche Pamfletten* (Amsterdam, 1858), nr. 15.

31 One copy is in the Brussels Royal Library. Typical is the annotation of the historian N. de Weert, who mentions in one line for the year 1535 Charles V's victories abroad and

were accused of the worst intentions; the whole verbose poem, of course, revolves around the Münsterite tragedy; the opening lines give evidence of his attitude: "Anabaptistae filii noctis" (Anabaptists, sons of the night). Typical of the views of government and of society at large, he fails to distinguish between revolutionary Anabaptists and the peaceful Mennonites. Whoever broke with the Catholic Church and accepted adult baptism became *ipso facto* a public enemy. Adult baptism was considered not merely an unacceptable dogmatic aberration, but rather a rallying point for all those who would without fail seize the first opportunity to destroy the existing political and social order and to introduce absolute anarchy.

Before the Reformation became a political issue, Anabaptism attracted little attention and executions were very rare. Hardly, however, had the first Anabaptists made their voice heard when the number of executions increased rapidly. And when the martyr lists are carefully studied, it is striking to note to what extent it was the Anabaptists who were the victims of the persecutions of the ecclesiastical and secular authorities. At Ghent, Bruges, and Courtrai, to mention only a few of the important centers of Reformation influence, the number of Anabaptist martyrs in the sixteenth century passes 70 per cent of those executed for non-Catholic thinking (the other 30 per cent consisted of Lutherans, Calvinists, iconoclasts, and people of unidentified religious convictions). The propagation of the Mennonite views went on therefore under extremely difficult conditions, since the short conversations in the workshop or in the street and the preaching in homes were extremely dangerous. Whoever became a Mennonite knew what he would face in case of arrest; no wonder that among the arrested Mennonites there were so few who recanted.

The mandates on heresy—more specifically on Anabaptism—were the cause not only of many executions but also of a first emigration.[32] Anyone who was aware that he was known as a Mennonite lost no time in placing himself beyond the reach of the authorities. So the first Flemish groups of Anabaptist exiles came into existence, opening the way for the later, more massive emigration. A few dozen refugees fled to England,

the fall of Münster. (*Chronycke van Nederland*, in Ch. Piot, *Chroniques de Brabant et de Flandre* [Brussels, 1879], p. 105.)

32 Besides the emigration which became inevitable, the mandates caused a certain apostasy. Wouter van Stoelwijk, arrested in 1538 and burned in Vilvoorde on March 24, 1541, declared: "May this be considered by all unfaithful Christians, who now return to the Roman Babel, from which they once separated, and make friends with the harlot they once hated; what can one say to such light-minded people: how can people, who once knew the truth, be so blind as to wander away from Christ Jesus, the only Saviour, and return to the shameful, cursed harlot of Babel?" (van Bracht, *Mirror*, II, pp. 55 f.)

but did not find there the expected haven, since there as well the government adopted measures to fight Anabaptism.

In London (once more the attraction of the big city asserted itself!) two Flemish Anabaptists and their wives were burned on November 23, 1538, while a third escaped the death penalty by abjuring his faith.[33] Hardly one and a half years later—April 10, 1540—London officers arrested a group of fifteen to twenty Anabaptist emigrants, consisting largely of Flemings.[34] On a larger scale there was emigration to the Northern Netherlands, a logical consequence of the close linguistic relationship. Most of them settled in the provinces of Holland and Zeeland, where not seldom they were accepted by the municipal labor institutions because of their technical skill.[35] The emigration, however, was not so general as to cause a collapse among the Mennonite groups of the province of Flanders.

Although the first congregations, presumably well established around 1545, could rejoice in having faithful and convinced members, they still lacked the binding element to build a strong fellowship in Flanders. As soon as they became conscious of their significance as a new—in their own view the only true—confessional group, an irresistible impulse arose to seek a closer co-operation between their several groups, just as their Northern Netherlands brethren had done. They saw the need for having someone to be constantly available to travel and visit all the Flemish congregations, to give them guidance, in particular in spiritual matters, but also in material problems. To have an elder (or bishop)—this is the name given to the leaders of the Anabaptist movement—from their own ranks became daily a more urgent necessity. An elder, however, was supposed to be a constant example of unquestionable purity in spirit and behavior and to show in the area of the faith an infallible knowledge. Such a man was not available in these relatively young congregations in

33 *Letters and Papers, Foreign and Domestic, of the Reign of Henry VIII* (London, 1893), p. 374. "Yesterday, the 22nd, Lambert, alias John Nycolsen, was burned in Smithfield and the same day two Flemings and one of their wives were adjudged to death. A third man abjured. They were Anabaptists."

34 *Ibid.*, XV, 1540 (London, 1896), p. 206. "[A certain Dr. Barnes] has been put in the tower with his two accomplices, accompanied by 10 or 12 burgesses of this town and 15 or 20 strangers, mostly from Flanders, and all Anabaptists."

35 J. K. van der Wulp, *Catalogus van de tractaten, pamphletten* . . . (Amsterdam, 1866-68), no. 23: "Memorandum of what seems, on the basis of divers information, to have happened in Amsterdam concerning the errors and sects of Lutheranism and Anabaptism and related matters." Article 39 is typical: "That others who fled from Flanders and Brabant settled in Amsterdam and that some of them as glovemakers and one as a bootlace maker got their wages from the municipal treasury." As regards the Flemish emigrants to Friesland, cf. A. M. Cramer, *Leven en verrichtingen van Menno Simons en over den oorsprong der Doopsgezinden voornamelijk in de Nederlanden* (Amsterdam, 1837), p. 37.

the period before 1550. The Anabaptists of the first period came in general from the working class. The converts had joined the new confession with enthusiasm, and with unbroken zeal they had appropriated the Mennonite doctrines. None of them, however, had the necessary schooling and the requisite spiritual strength to assume the leadership of the whole Flemish Mennonite brotherhood.

Hitherto the congregations had had to be satisfied with the visits of Northern elders, who rarely came through Flanders. Jan van Tricht (or Jan Matthijs van Middelburg),[36] Cornelis Claissone van Leiden,[37] and Gillis van Aken[38] were all too well known to the clerical and secular police to be able to allow themselves extended visits to any one town. If they visited Flanders at all, they made only a hasty circuit, spending a few days with the most important congregations to baptize the waiting converts.

As a result of the ever-increasing expansion of Mennonitism in Flanders the lack of permanent general leadership became more acute. About 1545 the problem was brought up in a meeting of Flemish brethren, perhaps at Ghent. The meeting, under its chairman Adriaan van Kortrijk, could do nothing but admit that the search in Flanders for someone meeting the requirements for the office of elder had been fruitless. It was therefore decided to send an appeal to the Antwerp (not the Northern Netherlands) brethren to ameliorate this deplorable lack by sending them a Southern Netherlands man. The text of this request, composed by the delegates of Ghent, Meenen, Roeselaere, Hondschoote, Nijpkerke, and Waasten, has been preserved undamaged. This extraordinarily important document follows:

Eternal, endless grace, love, fruit, peace, and mercy, from God our heavenly Father and His beloved Son Jesus Christ, who has washed us from our sins in His blood and has made us kings and priests; to God and His Father, to whom alone be glory and praise, honor and thanksgiving, from eternity to eternity. Amen.

Dearly beloved and cherished brethren, elders and ministers of the congregations at Antwerp; we, ministers of the congregations in Flanders, have been sincerely troubled and grieved by the great distress, trouble, and need which we observe and see in our congregations everywhere in that poor weak brethren tragically wander about like sheep without a shepherd; thus we may well lament and say that the harvest is great and the laborers are few.

36 Bruges City, *Bouc van den Steene, 1538-1539*, fol. 17vo.
37 Brussels Royal, *EA*, no. 34,877, fol. 208, Jan van den Vivere, *Chronycke van Gent* . . . , edited by F. de Potter (Ghent, 1885), February 17, 1554. *Memorieboek der Stad Gent*, ed., P. C. van der Meersch (Ghent, 1852-61), II, p. 273.
38 Gillis van Aken will be treated in the next chapter.

So following the counsel of Christ, the Lord of the harvest, we have prayed that He may send laborers into His harvest; nor have we left the matter there. We have been looking diligently among ourselves to find a man living in Flanders whom we with the consent of the congregations and your counsel could have put to the test, letting him have in all of Flanders the oversight of all the congregations, that we also might have an oversight over his behavior; and if, according to the testimony of our conscience, we might see a good, unquestionable behavior so that he could have inspired us with his behavior as well as with his teaching, then we would have requested you to install this man in the office of bishop. Since our search has not borne fruit, we are compelled, together with all the deacons of Flanders, to write to you, praying and fraternally requesting of your love that you may help us and send us for our assistance a man from your congregation, whom you may place over us in such a probationary ministry as we have described above.

Oh, dear brethren, consider our need; I hope that it is well known to many of you, for the congregations everywhere are young and have been visited seldom, and the devil, our adversary, visits us very sharply with manifold temptations, at times with the burdens of the flesh, at other times with heretical teachings. To protect us well against him we need sentinels who will blow the trumpets at the right time, and we have such a confidence in your love that you will not send us away uncomforted by you. So, dear brethren, do the best you can that we may be helped; "The grace of the Lord be with you" is our greeting. We have signed this as the ministers of all the congregations in Flanders.

Besides Adriaan van Kortrijk for Ghent, the letter was signed by the representatives of Meenen, Roeselaere, Hondschoote, and Nijpkerke; the delegate of Waasten did not sign.[39] The extant documents do not reveal whether the problem brought up by the Flemish Mennonite community was immediately solved by the Antwerp "council." It seems to me very doubtful that the Mennonites in Flanders could have had their own leaders before 1550; the first man to fill the difficult office of elder for Flanders was apparently Hans Busschaert (or Hans de Wever), a man who completely met the requirements. Not only was he one of their own district (although he actually was born in Dadizele), but above all he proved to be a righteous and dauntless leader. Hans Busschaert was, however, not active in Flanders until 1555; hence it may be concluded that the request remained unfulfilled for many years.

The fact, however, that Mennonitism could experience such expansion without the desired centralized leadership and in the midst of many dangers is in itself very significant. The accent in interpreting the above request should, in our opinion, not primarily fall on the admitted lack of a solid organization, but rather on the irrefutable proof that in

39 Brussels Royal, *EA*, no. 1191/10: "Affaires des religionnaires de Flandre."

spite of this lack Menno's faith had been spread throughout Flanders by 1550. It is no less interesting to notice in this document that the Flemish congregations during the first part of the sixteenth century lived in permanent contact with the congregation in cosmopolitan Antwerp. Antwerp had previously been known as the cradle of Dutch Lutheranism and also as an outstanding Calvinistic stronghold. Even so no elaborate argument is needed to picture Antwerp as a focus of Anabaptism. In its shelter the Anabaptist and later the Mennonite teachings developed rapidly. The interest of Jan van Geelen in this city, as an apostle of God's kingdom on earth, has already been mentioned. It may be significant that one of the seven medals worn by Jan van Leiden, the king of the Münsterites, had a picture of Antwerp on it.[40]

But also afterward, when the revolutionary chimeras were driven to the background, the Mennonite congregation had an opportunity to do constructive work under favorable conditions. Undoubtedly it had been possible even before 1540 to obtain a solid organization for the brotherhood in spite of the surveillance of the alert authorities, to which the numerous executions of Anabaptists by the municipal authorities testify.[41]

The greater security offered by Antwerp also made it possible for visiting Northern Netherlands elders to dwell here for longer periods unnoticed, which of course raised the local brotherhood in the estimation of the less privileged groups and thus procured for it a prominent position in the fold of the Southern Netherlands Mennonite brotherhood. Besides, the metropolis was of far-reaching importance for the Anabaptist groups as a distribution center for Reformation literature.[42]

In and after 1534 some peculiar writings appeared, which were

40 Brussels Royal, *Ms. divers,* no. 794/A, 748/A, fol. 192vo.

41 P. Génard, *AA,* XIV, pp. 12-17.

42 The following edict was issued in Antwerp on February 19, 1536: "Images, pictures, prints, or engravings of Jan van Leyden, calling himself King of Zion, executed at Münster, or of his accomplices; books containing the biographies of such heretics and delinquents are not to be sold; whosoever has such shall bring the same to the officers to be burned" (Génard, *op. cit.,* I, p. 201). The Antwerp authorities of course knew that the density of the city population stimulated Anabaptist immigration. Police checks were not lacking. On February 25, 1535, an order was issued that all Anabaptists had to leave the city before nightfall. (*Ibid.*) On June 14, 1535, the city authorities denied Anabaptists entry to the city and to that end established new guard sections. (*Ibid.,* p. 202.) The problem of the supervision of foreigners was always one of the chief difficulties which kept the goal, the elimination of Mennonite immigrants, unattainable. On November 5, 1550, on order of the emperor, the following edict was issued: "Foreigners suspected of heresies, and in particular of the sect of the Anabaptists, are not to be admitted here without an attestation from the parish of their last place of residence." Still more drastic—emergency necessitated ever sharper measures—was the ordinance of February 3, 1558: "Foreigners having lived here less than two years are to leave; exiled persons from foreign countries must present the documents concerning their banishment."

very much sought after by the Northern Anabaptists and with which the South as well was probably well supplied, though the documents now available do not throw a clear light on the matter. In the course of that year Adriaan van Berghen published *Een profitellic ende troostelic boexken van den gheloove ende hoope, wat dat oprechte ghelove is. Ende welcke ghenade die menschen doer het ghelove vercrigen. Ende hoe scadelicken dat ongheloove is. Noch een boexken van die liefde die god tot ons heeft, en wat liefde werct, ende hoe schadelic die liefde des werelts is, allen menschen seer troostelic.* (A Helpful and Encouraging Book on Faith and Hope, What True Faith Is. What Grace Man May Receive by Faith. And How Harmful Unbelief Is. Another Book on the Love God Has Toward Us, and How Harmful Love for the World Is; Very Helpful for Everyone.) Another Antwerp publication in the same spirit was *Van dat gheloove aen onsen salichmaker Jesum Christum, wat onbegrijpelijke verdiensten, ende heylicheyt ende salicheyt we daer doer verkrijghen. Ende van eens christen menschen offeninghe, ende wercken.* (Of Faith in Our Saviour Jesus Christ and What Inconceivable Merits, Holiness, and Blessedness We Thereby Receive. Further Concerning the Expressions and the Works of a Christian.)

Jan Claeszen—later hanged at Amsterdam—declared in 1544 that he had had 600 copies of Menno's writings printed at Antwerp; his statement that he had distributed 200 in Holland and the rest in Friesland by no means proves that out of this large edition he did not dispose of several dozen copies in the South.[43]

Focal point of Mennonite spiritual life, preferred residence of the most prominent leaders, center for the publication and distribution of writings—all this brought the congregation in Antwerp to the fore. It is consequently not surprising that the Flemish congregations, which had to do without all these privileges, turned for help to the Antwerp "mother" group in the hope of becoming able to take an independent position in the second half of the sixteenth century. However unfinished the task may have been, yet in this period before 1550 the solid foundations were laid which made it possible for Mennonitism, after the mid-century, to withstand over a long period the heavy blows which it was obliged to endure from its embittered adversaries.

---

43 Grete Grosheide, *Bijdrage tot de Geschiedenis der Anabaptisten in Amsterdam* (Hilversum, 1938), p. 149.

II. GROWTH AND STRUGGLE
1550-1576

At the beginning of the second half of the sixteenth century Mennonitism was irresistibly becoming the largest non-Catholic confession in Flanders. There, where the Mennonite brotherhood had victoriously defied the merciless edicts, Lutheranism lost much of its prestige, to regain a considerable importance in the Reformation of the Southern Netherlands only after 1565, and then primarily in Antwerp and vicinity.

To be sure, the Northern Netherlands church historian, W. J. Pont, gave quite a different picture of the situation in his time: he asserted that the pure Lutheran spirit was to be found nowhere in the Southern Netherlands before 1546. We know now that Pont's opinion was incorrect; his false picture may be attributed to his inadequate archival research. Pont's approach is already dubious when he accuses all the existing Lutheran congregations in Flanders and the other Southern Netherlands provinces of never having really accepted Luther's views. Still less acceptable is Pont's assertion that there is not a single archival document that can disprove his thesis.[1] The very fact that historical research on the Reformation in the period before 1550 is still far from complete suffices to make us view with suspicion such a claim, and documents in the Bruges archives have in fact already refuted it. According to these sources, Hector van Dommele, Maertin de Smet, and Antheunis van der Cloet had actually accepted Lutheranism ever since 1524-25 and had taught in the spirit of the great reformer. Erasmus van der Eecke crowned this purely Lutheran tradition by publishing several hundred copies of an apology for Luther.

However, little came of this promising start. Lutheranism was outrun by about 1530, first by the radical Anabaptist movement, afterward by the Mennonite movement.

Calvinism first appeared in the person of Pierre Brully around Tournai,[2] but did not prosper before 1550, even in cities like Bruges and Ghent.[3] Since the civil and ecclesiastical authorities in 1550 and the following years had no serious cases of Calvinistic agitation to deal with,

---

1 Cf. Verheyden, *Bruges*, p. 13 f.

2 Charles Paillard, *Le procès de Pierre Brully (1544-1595)* (Paris, 1878).

3 In Verheyden, *Ghent*, pp. 5 ff., we have explained in detail why the following of Martin Hueribloc in 1545 can hardly be considered a Calvinist congregation.

their attention was caught all the more by the increasing spread of Mennonite teachings, in the cities as well as in the rural areas. That this expansion disturbed even the highest governmental authorities becomes evident in their lively interest in the arrival of Jan van Sol in Brussels.

Jan van Sol was born at Dordrecht, but left the Netherlands in 1530 because of debts and settled in Danzig. Even before his flight he revealed himself to the Amsterdam authorities as a zealous opponent of Anabaptism by betraying the plot of Hendrik van Hasselt. After some years in Danzig, he had the bitter experience of increasing hostility in return for his anti-Mennonite activities. The constant disapproval of his ungrateful fellow countrymen became such a heavy burden that at the beginning of 1549 Jan van Sol decided to return to his homeland and to offer to the government there his experience and his services in combating the Anabaptist menace. In the summer of the same year he appeared before the Amsterdam authorities and submitted to them an ambitious project.

Since, however, the practical realization of van Sol's project lay beyond the competency of the municipal or the provincial authorities, his proposals were sent on December 8, 1550, to Viglius, president of the Secret Council. As a result van Sol was granted an interview on December 22 of the same year with J. de Wierden, secretary to the emperor. De Wierden not only accepted the written plan, but used this opportunity to ask for information concerning the organization of the Mennonite communities. De Wierden was not disappointed; van Sol's report included, besides well-known generalities, many details worth knowing. He saw in Anabaptism three well-defined movements, the Melchiorites (the peaceful Mennonite group), the Davidites (after the teachings of David Joris, seldom heard of in the Southern Netherlands), and the Batenburgers. Of these three groups—Jan van Sol continued—the first one was the most important. The movement was under the leadership of Obbe and Dirk Philips, as well as of Menno Simons (the only one of significance for Flanders). These leaders sent out teachers, who preferred to enter a town by night and were immediately brought to a safe hiding place by some fellow believers.

Van Sol described furthermore the important function of "purse-bearers," deacons charged with the financial affairs of the congregations. Very interesting is his statement that these deacons made loans to the less fortunate brethren, who returned the borrowed funds as soon as they were able. According to van Sol, this practice was the only explanation for the fact that ever more well-to-do people were to be found in Mennonite circles.

Following his interview with Jan van Sol, de Wierden copied in his

report some important points of the proposed plan for the elimination of
the Anabaptist activities. This summary indicates that the heaviest task
was to be given to the municipal authorities, namely, to gather information both about those staying within their jurisdiction and about those
leaving town. It is remarkable that in van Sol's project the ecclesiastical
authorities are mentioned only exceptionally; they were to help the
government by granting or refusing to the suspect an attestation of good
Catholic behavior; otherwise they would be called upon only for more
thorough theological examination in dubious cases.

The next day, December 24, 1550, Jan van Sol again appeared before
de Wierden. The interview brought few new facts to light, except for
the passages where the man of Dordrecht spoke about the development
of the Mennonite brotherhoods in Danzig. Explicitly he assured the
imperial secretary that the Dutch Anabaptists were not unwelcome there,
because the authorities saw in their immigration a profitable affair. Not
only did the Dutch immigrants spontaneously offer not less than thirty
guilders' rent instead of the usual four, but beyond that their working
methods resulted in an undeniable improvement in the local agricultural
and textile industries; these changes were, of course, regarded very
favorably by the Danzig authorities.

The case of Jan van Sol finally came before the jurist Veltwyck, a
member of the Secret Council, who, after asking for and receiving more
details about the person of the witness, proceeded with an exact juridical
examination of his project, which was drawn up in sixteen articles.

The first four points, concerning the problem of baptism, Veltwyck
considered solid and appropriate. He agreed absolutely—assuming the
approval of the theologians of Louvain—with the requirement that a
child should be baptized within twenty-four hours after its birth in the
presence of its father, who himself should apply for this ecclesiastical
ceremony. If the father happened not to be at home at that moment, he
should immediately upon his return go to the priest to express his thanks
for the intervention by the church. The mother also should after her
recovery go to the priest, who would admit her to the church again after
the purification ceremonies.

In contrast with these four articles the fifth one was unacceptable to
Veltwyck. Van Sol proposed to obligate the parents to see to it that two
neighbors would be present as witnesses at every childbirth. This measure,
Veltwyck said, would be practical only when both parents and neighbors belonged to the same class, but was absolutely to be rejected in case
of noble or wealthy families. For they would not be at all pleased with
the idea of having to invite to the childbed less well-to-do neighbors, to
say nothing of people of other classes.

On the sixth and the seventh points of the project Veltwyck had no objections. Every citizen would be required to inform a district officer immediately of the news of a childbirth, and everyone above the age of twelve was to be required to receive the Holy Sacrament at least once a year.

Where Jan van Sol in his eighth article returned to the social realm his proposals were again blocked by the refusal of Veltwyck. The plan advocated the division of villages and small towns into four parts, so that everyone, regardless of rank, could be subjected to thorough surveillance. The jurist replied that such a project was impracticable, since the priests and all those who by special privilege escaped municipal jurisdiction would certainly not submit to requirements of this kind. Nor was it feasible to oblige every citizen who had temporarily left his town or village to go to the priest within three days after his return to receive the Holy Sacrament (Article 9), since the church itself would not agree.

With the rejection of the eighth and ninth articles, the tenth lost most of its significance. It called for the neighbors of a fugitive to report his absence from home immediately to the authorities and, in case the emigrant returned, to check exactly whether he lived up to the regulations of the preceding two articles. Of this proposal there remained, of course, only the obligatory report of absence, which in itself was not without value since it would lighten the task of the district officers.

In the eleventh point Jan van Sol explained his suggestion that the wedding ceremony should no longer be performed before a limited circle, but publicly by the clergy. Against this Veltwyck argued that such a change of custom would be unacceptable to the clergy, though the proposal undoubtedly would be useful in combating the plague of secret weddings. The plan won Veltwyck's consent when the requirement was added that if a husband or wife left the country, the abandoned partner should immediately inform the authorities. They would have to report to the central government all the information gathered concerning the fugitives, and the court would in turn notify the municipal authorities of the town where the emigrant was expected to settle.

Concerning the twelfth article no agreement could be reached. It proposed that in the future the owners of houses should take prospective renters to the authorities to have them state why they had left their former residence and for what reason they needed a new dwelling. Too difficult to apply, ruled the jurist; right from the start there would be a conflict with the merchants, to whom freedom of movement was of the highest importance.

The next article was just as unreasonable; if it were to be executed to the letter, everyone who had settled in a town after 1534 would have

4

to secure within one month an attestation from his former place of residence, sworn to by three or four witnesses. The note Veltwyck wrote in the margin was the laconic "absolutely impracticable." We find the same reaction to the fourteenth point, which called for renewal of all such attestations issued before the end of 1550.

Thus far van Sol's project was not especially directed against the Anabaptists. This lack, however, was compensated by the fifteenth article, which, if executed, would be a powerful weapon in the hands of clerical and worldly authorities. It called for an obligatory oath of loyalty to the customs and laws of the city, after the suspect had first cleared the matter of his attestation. To a Mennonite this obstacle was insuperable, since an oath was forbidden for him. However promising this means to suppress Anabaptism may have seemed to Veltwyck, he was compelled to reject it. Once more the merchant class would be the main obstacle, since one could not ask merchants, who came from so many different regions, to take an oath of loyalty again at the entrance of every city.

Consideration for the merchants also prevented the realization of the proposals of the sixteenth and last article, which specified that refugees who sought to return to the Netherlands should be permitted to do so only with the approval of the competent sovereign courts. As for emigrants suspected of Anabaptism who did not return, their goods would immediately be confiscated, half of the proceeds returned to the family and the other half given to the imperial treasury. Veltwyck appended to these final propositions the following annotation: "This article would be very useful were it not for the diversity of the sects and for those who frequent the country as merchants." Besides his explicit desire to take measures which would reach not only the Anabaptists but all sectarians, the leading motive for rejection was again the protection of the merchants.

This document was sent by the Secret Council to Ruard Tapper on January 2, 1551, with the request to have it discussed by the theologians of Louvain. The answer from Louvain was favorable, but the attitude taken by the Council of Holland, Zeeland, and Friesland toward the van Sol project was less reassuring. Concerning the articles about making public the baptismal ceremony, this Northern Netherlands authority pointed out that even many Catholics were eager to keep certain births as secret as possible.

On the problem of refugees the attitude of the Dutch Council was still more categorical. It was vigorously argued that the economy of the Northern Netherlands was dependent primarily on commerce; consequently it would be absolutely indefensible on a mere suspicion to confiscate the goods of merchants who left for Germany or Norway for four or five years if before leaving they were known to be good Catholics. Furthermore, the proposed measures against legitimately suspected emigrants were superfluous, since these were provided for by the edicts of January 18 and September 25, 1550.[4]

Looking for a moment ahead of events, we should remark that the reserve of the central government and the numerous objections of the provincial authorities softened with time. The numerous confiscation lists which were made up after Duke Alva arrived and the obligatory oath of fidelity to the Spanish regime imposed after the restoration of the Hapsburg authority by Alessandro Farnese, proved that van Sol's proposals were useful.

Though van Sol's plan did not arouse an immediate tightening of the stringency of surveillance, yet shortly after 1550 a savage storm of persecution broke out over a number of cities in the Flemish province. Limiting ourselves here to the Mennonite victims of this persecution in the years 1551-53 who are now known we may name: in Courtrai,[5] Jooskint: in Bruges,[6] Jan Helleman; in Ghent,[7] Margriete van den Berghe, Gooris Cooman, Naentgen Bornaige, Wouter van der Weyden, Catharina van Lier, Hansken Buefkin, Hans van Overdam, Pieter van den Hende, Willem de Camp, Jacob Curick, Willem de Brouwere, Gillis van Gusseme, Lysbette Piersins, Pieter van Olmen, Cornelis Claissone, Willem van Leuven, Lievin Verreken; in Komen, Guilliame van Robaeys and an anonymous blacksmith;[8] in Oostende, Wouter van Capelle.[9] Jacob and Philippus de Heere had to leave Aalst in great haste to avoid falling into the hands of the court because of their too open teaching activity.[10]

The urgent tone of Jan van Sol's proposals demonstrates that the expansion of the Mennonites had become a problem for the fearful Catholic population as well as for the highest civil authorities. The martyrs mentioned provide eloquent evidence for the effective inner flowering of the Mennonite groups, as their statements during the trials amply confirm.

---

4 Brussels Royal, *EA*, no. 1171/3.

5 Theodor Sevens, *Handvesten rakende de Wederdoopers ende Calvinisten der XVIe eeuw in de voormalige kastelnij van Kortrijk* (Courtrai, 1924), p. 86.

6 Cf. Verheyden, *Bruges*.

7 Cf. Verheyden, *Ghent*.

8 Van Braght, *Mirror*, II, pp. 105, 183.

9 *Ibid.*, p. 150.

10 J. Loosjes, "Jan Jacobsz en de Jan Jacobsgezinden," in F. Pijper, *Nederlandsch archief voor Kerkgeschiedenis*, n.s., XI (1914), p. 186. The de Heerle brothers established at Harlingen the first cotton and linen weaving mill.

Before 1550 few names of well-known minister-teachers reach us; but in the period at hand, 1550-75, we find many active personalities. It is true that the actual leaders, Menno Simons and Dirk Philips, never dared to be personally active in Flanders, but these Northerners saw to it that the Flemish field was not deprived of spiritual leadership and material help. In addition the Northern Netherlands sent a dauntless worker in the person of Leenaert Bouwens.[11] He had joined the leadership of the Northern brotherhood at a time when it urgently needed competent helpers.

As a result of regrettable developments the places of Obbe Philips and David Joris had become vacant by 1540, while the remaining elders, Menno Simons and Dirk Philips, had had to take refuge abroad, the former in Emden and Holstein, the latter in Danzig.

Between 1542 and 1547 the brotherhood ordained five new teachers: Adam Pastor, Hendrik van Vreden, Antonius van Keulen, Frans Reines de Cuyper, and Gillis van Aken. About the same time Teunis van Hastenrath filled the office of preacher in the Ruhr area. Leenaert Bouwens, after serving as an evangelist for many years, was ordained an elder in 1553 by Menno Simons. The next year he began to teach and to baptize in the Southern Netherlands. In the words of his convert Jacques d'Auchy, "He taught amendment of life, putting off the old man and putting on the new one." This first trip by Bouwens lasted until 1556. He stayed mainly in Antwerp, Brussels, Tournai, Ghent, Ypres, Courtrai, Mechelen, and Meenen, and added to the Southern brotherhood 225 baptized members, as reported in his diary (baptismal list). Bouwens' activities were however not limited to baptizing those who had requested it; beyond that he urged the ablest among them to preach.[12]

Especially for Flanders the recruitment of new elements for the propagation of the faith was of the highest importance. Even more than the great number of brethren who joined, thanks to Bouwens' activities, these new missionaries—though their names are not known—laid the groundwork for the success which Mennonitism was soon to have in the Southern Netherlands. Equally fruitful were Bouwens' visits to Flanders in the periods 1557-61 and 1563-65, during which his baptismal lists for the South were extended with 367 new names.

However, Bouwens stopped his fiery preaching and his successful

---

11 W. J. Kühler, *op. cit.*, pp. 279, 293, 301, 306, 311 f., 317-24, 328, 331, 349, 357, 364, 369, 395-404, 414, 421 f., 427, 432, 434. Vos, *DtA*, pp. 333-37, 390.

12 V. P., *Successio (B.R.N.)*, II, p. 51): "[Bouwens] was so active in his false office that he seduced many in several provinces, such as Friesland, Overijssel, Holland, Zeeland, Brabant, and Flanders, *ordaining to the ministry many who with him spread the evil seed* (italics ours)."

baptizing in the South after 1565 to devote all his powers to the guidance of the Northern brotherhood. Stubborn enemy of every compromise in matters of exact application of the doctrines in everyday life, he soon came into conflict with Menno Simons, advocate of a wholesome tolerance. With the help of Dirk Philips, Bouwens embittered the last years of Menno's life, not only pushing him mercilessly out of the leadership but also forcing him to make concessions with which he did not really agree.

The new leaders, whose position was uncontested after Menno's death on January 31, 1561, bore the heavy responsibility for the tragic divisions in the Northern brotherhood and for an indisputable stiffening of Mennonite doctrines. In Flanders Bouwens never succeeded in bringing the name and theology of Menno Simons into discredit, as is clear from the testimony of Martin Micron, who pictures Menno's influence in Belgium as predominating. Neither was Bouwens able to stir up warm sympathy for his exaggerated disciplinary action in the Mennonite groups. Undoubtedly he used his travels in the years 1557-61 and 1563-65 to seek a following for his conceptions, but because of the strict control by civil and clerical authorities,[13] his visits in the Flemish cities were too short to have far-reaching results. Furthermore the Southern congregations were too busy with the common struggle for existence to listen to the dangerous advice of Bouwens.

In spite of the great number of people Bouwens baptized, his name appears only rarely in trials, letters, and other records. These rare notices are never accompanied by bitter remarks about his life and work. This, however, cannot be said of Gillis van Aken,[14] who in spite of his numerous baptisms did not enjoy a reputation for holiness after 1555. His life can hardly be called an example of virtue and perseverance. Only a few years after his ordination as elder, in 1554, he had to withdraw from his office because of adultery involving sisters of the congregation. He, however, showed sincere remorse and pledged most solemnly to fulfill his duties worthily in the future, if he were given a new chance. His plea to be allowed once more to fill the elder's office was granted by Menno Simons, who, with the consent of Bouwens and Dirk Philips (whose tolerance is less understandable), rehabilitated the penitent sinner.

13 An Antwerp edict of December 20, 1558, referred directly to him and Joachim Vermeeren: "Whoever delivers or denounces one of these two rebaptizers so that they can be arrested, the same shall receive from the city three hundred carolus-guilders and furthermore shall be amnestied if he is an Anabaptist" (Génard, *AA*, II, p. 355).

14 K. Vos, *Menno Simons* (Leiden, 1914), pp. 96, 98, *et passim; DtA*, p. 337; W. J. Kühler, *op. cit.*, pp. 262, 279, 300, 306, 313, *et passim*.

After Gillis van Aken had had to admit that his preaching in the North had little success he went to Southern Netherlands. Here his activity left many traces: not only was his presence reported in the most widely spread and the most isolated towns, but he also did much for the expansion of the Flemish brotherhood by his numerous baptisms. On this point the text of his sentence leaves no doubt. This document actually says: "The defendant [Gillis van Aken] has been rebaptized and has held several conventicles in several places, and was the cause of many people being drawn into error."

And yet after Gillis' death the brethren could not look back on his career with gratitude, for he showed great cowardice before his judges after his arrest in Antwerp in 1555. Overwhelmed by the fear of an almost inevitable death sentence he immediately recanted; indeed, he declared himself willing to return to all the places he had formerly visited and to confess his error publicly. Yet all these humiliations did not suffice to bring about his release, since the Antwerp government did not intend to lose this rare chance to execute an "Anabaptistarum Episcopus" (the title found in the margin of the sentence). Consequently Gillis van Aken was beheaded on July 10, 1557. After his execution, his right hand was cut off and exhibited on a wheel outside the city.

To the Mennonites, who in the words of Jeronimus Segertsz would "rather be tortured ten times a day than to forsake the faith which I have confessed,"[15] the cowardly attitude of Gillis was a great disappointment. Vincken Verwee, who knew that by recanting she could mitigate her sentence, nevertheless did not hesitate one moment with her statement: "It would grieve her to die as he [Gillis van Aken] had died, for he forsook his faith."[16]

The confidence of the Flemish brotherhood in their leaders was again sorely tried some years later by Joachim Vermeeren's[17] disgraceful denial of his faith. An active propagandist of Menno's teachings, he baptized many in Flanders during the period 1557-60. His activity as baptizer can be traced with certainty in Meenen in 1557[18] and Ghent in 1558.[19] The result was that already in December, 1558, three hundred carolus-guilders were promised to any who would deliver the "dangerous

15 Van Braght, Mirror, II, p. 125. A similar report comes from Courtrai: Jooskint declared to his inquisitor, "For I trust the Lord so strongly that I am confident that He will guard the door of my mouth, so that I shall tell you nothing, even if you should tear me to pieces" (Offer des Heeren, 1566 edition, fol. 141vo, B.R.N., II, 223).

16 Bruges City, Bouc van den Steene, 1558-1559, fol. 90vo.

17 Vos, DtA, pp. 339-44.

18 Ibid., p. 343.

19 Ibid.

baptizer" into the hands of the authorities. Neither this serious threat nor his wife's imprisonment in a dungeon by the Antwerp government in May, 1559, could keep Joachim (de Suikerbakker, i.e., the Pastry Cook as he was called by the Flemish Mennonites) from continuing his baptizing in the Southern Netherlands. In 1565, however, his courageous apostolate was suddenly terminated. He was at that time with the Mennonites in Cologne, and with a group of fellow believers, among them the Elder Matthijs, fell into the hands of the local magistrates. Less bloodthirsty than the corresponding institutions in Flanders, the authorities in Cologne tried to bring the prisoners back to the Catholic Church. This strategy was fatal for Joachim Vermeeren's influence, for he, who had been the leader of the Flemish Mennonites, surrendered soon to the persuasive talents of the Cologne theologian George Cassander. Though he escaped thus from an otherwise inevitable death sentence, he was irrevocably lost to the Mennonites.

Besides these three very well-known Anabaptist leaders in the period before 1560, the Fleming Hans Busschaert, called de Wever (the Weaver), should be noted.[20] He was ordained an elder by Menno Simons in 1555 and chose the South as his chief field of labor, only rarely attending the leaders' conferences in the North, where he always persistently advocated Flemish tolerance in matters of discipline. Since Busschaert's main activity can be traced only after 1560, we shall return later to a more extensive discussion of his work.

The most remarkable achievement in the years 1550-60 was certainly the establishment of closer contact between the elders and the congregations. Besides the important but yet only temporary appearances of Leenaert Bouwens, we notice now the almost permanent presence in the Flemish country of Gillis van Aken, Joachim Vermeeren, and finally of Hans de Wever. This new step caused a remarkable change in congregational life. Urged by these evangelists to study to be more fit for the battle against the "heathen" environment, simple workmen felt obliged to learn to read and write. That they accomplished this feat is amply proved by the few trial records, letters, and hymns which have been preserved.

---

20 *Ibid.*, pp. 354-56. He led several meetings in Ghent, baptized often, and performed many wedding ceremonies. Because of the alertness of the Ghent authorities it was impossible for him to reside in the city. Yet in spite of every difficulty this undaunted apostle remained in constant contact with the brethren living here. Here as elsewhere the brethren and sisters maintained a stubborn silence when the inquisitors sought to determine the identity of their leaders. This explains why hardly any names of teachers of this important congregation have been recorded. The only one named was one Hendrik of Arnhem "with the crippled foot." It became known that he administered baptism to Martynkin Meere and Belynkin de Jaghere in the presence of some twenty believers.

So it cannot be considered miraculous when in their defense against the priests in charge of their trials these simple people speak, as the documents testify, the language of initiates; or when in their correspondence with fellow believers they reveal a style which testifies to a highly developed gift for expression. Though the spring from which they draw is always the same, the Bible, yet in their speaking and writing there is not mere mechanical reproduction, but knowledge demonstrating an indisputably high capacity for assimilation of Biblical truth. Around the faithful citation of texts from the Holy Scriptures (especially when defending their doctrines), the living water of their personal experiences always comes richly to the surface.

Typical of these "self-made preachers" was Hans van Overdam,[21] who went to the stake at Ghent on July 9, 1551. Because of his important function in the Ghent brotherhood, we shall discuss him at some length. It is not improbable that this man from Ghent was a member of the first Mennonite group in his city. He rapidly became so ardent and fearless an advocate of Menno's teachings that in 1545 he barely escaped arrest by the police. He probably took refuge in Antwerp, but that could not keep him from now and then visiting his former field of labor. He was present among the restless crowd which on April 11 attended the execution of Margriete van den Berghe, Jooris Cooman, Wouter van der Weyden, and Naentgen Bornaige, four converts of Gillis van Aken.[22]

It is not accidental that Hans was present at this execution. These martyrs had been baptized by Gillis van Aken upon his recommendation. As soon as their imprisonment became known, he repeatedly asked the Antwerp congregation to remember the prisoners in their prayers, that they might be steadfast in their faith to the bitter end. Thus Hans van Overdam was present in the crowd which had flocked together to satisfy its lust for sensation. Let us observe the scene as described in the records.

Naentgen had hardly given her last testimony with the words, "This is the day I've been longing for,"[23] when Jooris Cooman raised his voice amidst the roaring flames, saying: "Remember that we do not die for theft, murder, or heresy!" Still more sensational was the testimony of

21 Ghent State, *RVSC*, 1549-54, fol. 160; *RVBW*, reg. 20, fol. 84; *Serie F*, No. 21, item 3. Van Braght, *Mirror*, II, pp. 86-94.

22 Van Braght, *Mirror*, II, p. 106.

23 Grietgen had already called out, on seeing the stakes, "My lords, you can save three stakes; we will all four die on one, for we are already one in spirit" *(ibid.)*. Maeyken Doornaerts gave the same kind of testimony at the stake at Belle in 1556; she actually addressed the crowd: "This is the hour I have been longing for, to make an end to all my suffering." Friar Cornelis was later to picture the courage of the Mennonites at the place of execution: "Bah! they go singing, laughing, yea dancing and leaping to meet their death, yea right into the searing fire" *(Broer Cornelis*, p. 230).

Wouter van der Weyden, when he affirmed Cooman's words: "You citizens of Ghent, we do not suffer like heretics and Lutherans, a glass of beer in one hand and the Testament in the other, thus dishonoring God's Word and handling it in drunkenness, but we die for the righteous truth." In vain the monks tried to silence them. When the inquisitor Titelman tried to speak to the people before the scaffold, shouts arose: "You mad antichrists, stand aside and let them speak."[24]

Was Hans van Overdam, if not the author, at least the instigator of these popular manifestations? It may very well be the case in view of his activity during the next days, during which he campaigned powerfully against the clergy and government of Ghent. They had succeeded in persuading three young people, who had been arrested together with those executed on April 11, to return to the Catholic Church. Convinced that this apostasy had become possible only through unjust coercion practiced by the local authorities upon insufficiently prepared brethren, Hans van Overdam drew up a sharp manifesto, of which he had "a brother who can write better than I" make six copies, and posted it at different points in the town. In merciless language he made serious charges against the clergy. "Woe unto you, troops of Antichrist, who put on the ancient customs of the Roman Church like armor to defend yourself against the truth, who use the imperial edicts as a shield, and who wield the sword of the state to shed innocent blood in every land." "Oh, you spiritual Babel, how shall the Lord visit vengeance upon you for the innocent souls and the blood of His witnesses, of which He finds you guilty. You have made the kings of the earth and all the nations drunk with the wine of spiritual adultery, so that they cannot hear nor see the truth." In equally harsh words, after vigorously rejecting any revolutionary ideas, he attacks the Ghent magistracy. "Take account, noble Lords, of this abuse and mishandling of your estate and office; we confess it to be not of God, but of the devil. And Antichrist [the Catholics] has bewitched you and blinded your eyes with devilish cunning, that you yourselves are no longer responsible."

The same line of thought can be found in the song of the Ghent martyrs of 1551[25] (Hans van Overdam himself was one of them), where

---

24 For Claes de Praet, who also was in the crowd, this incident became the occasion of conversion. Arrested in 1556, he in his turn had to appear before Titelman. The chief inquisitor used the opportunity to compare his arrests with pulling weeds in the field of the faithful. He must have been startled by the response: "Five years ago when you planted those four stakes on the Verle Square and stood on the scaffold and preached, the people said, 'The Antichrist is preaching!' I began to ask what kind of faith those people died so courageously for, and I searched the Scriptures" (B.R.N., II, pp. 238-53).

25 B.R.N., II, pp. 516 ff.

the poet exclaims: "O Magistrates, awake; how long would ye be blind?/ How awful it is that ye would ignore/Him who entrusted to you the carnal sword./Those whom you murder are precious to Christ."

Asked why he personally had not defended his fellow believers before the authorities, Hans van Overdam answered: "The world may call the sheep a long time before they come, since they know that he will kill them with great cruelty, without justice or reason." In his unshakable conviction of the indisputable superiority of the Mennonite teachings over all the other existing faiths, he did not shrink from proposing to the government a public debate between the most able representatives of the Catholics and some Anabaptist leaders, on the condition that the latter would receive the necessary guarantees of personal safety. The loser in the debate thus organized was to be burned at the stake! Sharply Hans van Overdam added to this sensational proposal: "But your hooded ones [monks] would tremble too much if they had to debate with me at the risk of the stake."[26] This "ordeal by fire" motif is hardly original, but finds its source no doubt in Hans van Overdam's Bible knowledge; he was probably thinking of the epic scene where Elijah confronted the priests of Baal before King Ahab. I Kings 18.

The naive challenge of this manifesto brought no results except a more active search for this dangerous Mennonite spokesman. In spite of the increased risk he remained in the city for some time; he was finally trapped with a group of fellow believers just as he was planning to return to Antwerp. He had wanted to address the brethren and sisters in Ghent one last time before his departure to the capital. To that end he charged the messengers whose task it was to invite the members to a meeting to announce a farewell meeting for the next day in the woods of St. Antelinks (near Aalst). As he appeared at the appointed place in the early morning with his closest friend, Hans Buefkin, he saw to his surprise that there was not a single member of the congregation present. His surprise was short-lived, however, for presently the bailiffs of St. Pieter (Ghent) and of Aalst appeared on the scene and told him that the others had already fallen into the trap. The meeting—as became clear during the trial—had been betrayed "by a Judas, who was among us and who seemed to be the most pious brother of all."

Because Hans and his brethren had been caught within the jurisdiction of the Aalst bailiff, the officers led them to a castle in the vicinity. The same day the imprisoned Mennonites received many calls from fearless fellow believers. The court investigation was begun at St. Antelinks,

---

26 Seldom did a Mennonite speak so boldly at his trial. Well known is the outburst of Claes de Praet (1556) against the clergy present at his trial (cited above, pp. 13 f.).

but the actual hearings had to be held in Ghent, since the trap had been laid by the Ghent government, which, however, had little interest in organizing the trial. The regent, Margaret of Parma, had to intervene in the case and oblige the municipal authorities of Ghent to take charge. As a result the prisoners had to be transported to the city. At their departure from the castle Hans and the others were encouraged by his sister-in-law and another unknown brother. The officers caught both of them and put them on the wagon. A little farther on, another woman shared their fate for saying to the transported, "God keep you." About noon the group reached Ghent, where meanwhile a large crowd had assembled, of whom not a few demonstrated their sympathy with the victims. Hans van Overdam said, "If they had arrested all who addressed us, they would have needed more than twenty wagons."

The questioning itself, in so far as it left the field of faith and aimed at gaining information about the organization of the congregation, had no results, in spite of the fact that Hans van Overdam and others had to appear before the judges as many as five times. The investigators often had a hard time. When one of the clergymen, enraged by the stubborn defense of the Mennonites, exclaimed: "Fools, fools, heretics, heretics, that's what you are," he was immediately answered by van Overdam: "Look there, isn't he a fine teacher? Paul says that a teacher should not be quarrelsome nor angry!"

After such an attitude there could be no question about the fate of this fervent Mennonite. With him eleven other Mennonites were executed in 1551, a particularly heavy blow for the brotherhood in Ghent.

Limiting ourselves here for a moment to Ghent, we are struck by the fact that beginning with these draconic measures in 1551 the local authorities left no stone unturned to fight heresy and even took measures which were not directly prescribed by the edicts. For instance, the city allotted important sums of money to the clergy to recruit new teachers who would be specially trained to combat the "excesses." In 1553 Franchois van Nieuland received 16£ 13 s. 4 d. gr. to send four or five young people to Louvain to have them educated "in the divine learning that they afterwards may become in this city spiritual helpers, chaplains, and pastors to extinguish the errors and heresies now prevailing." At the same time the Franciscan monastery was allowed 10 s. gr. for the expenses of a meeting held on October 10, 1553, "to find out whether among them and their hired attendants the Word of God and the Holy Scriptures were rightly interpreted and preached, according to the teachings of the Holy Christian Church to keep far from all errors and heresies."[27]

27 Ghent City, *Stadsrekeningen*, 1553-54, fol. 201.

Repeatedly the Council of Flanders, the city governments, and the clergy were urged not to relax their zeal in persecuting the non-Catholics. It is not strange that, besides numerous lighter sentences, no less than twenty-five Protestants, among them nineteen Mennonites, were put to death.

Bruges, Courtrai, and all of Southern Flanders showed an identical picture in the mid-century. One result of this general wave of repression was that many Flemish Mennonites fled from the province and found refuge in Dordrecht, Leiden, Amsterdam, Emden, and other Dutch cities. Among those who reached Amsterdam and fell into the hands of the law were Jan de Monick, who called himself Fernando van Ghendt, Lourens Nettenszn, Lievijn van Gent, Jan Janszn, and Meyntgen van Brugge. Stijntje Evertsdr van Deventer may also be mentioned here since she had left Leiden for Ghent before 1550 and left Ghent only at the beginning of the persecution. At Leiden Adriaen Cornelisz admitted that shortly before his arrest he had been in Flanders.[28]

According to Claes de Praet—executed in Ghent in 1556—many citizens of Ghent must have been hiding at Emden.[29] Equally unsafe was Antwerp, since Annetgen Muliers (perhaps related to Willem Mulier, the first Mennonite to be executed in Ghent, on July 15, 1535), Truyken Boens, Lijnken, Anneken Boens, and Barbara Thielemans left Antwerp for Amsterdam. Jeronimus van der Capellen and his wife were less fortunate. They left Ghent because his activity had been noticed, and since then they had been hiding in Antwerp, where they were arrested early in 1557 and executed.[30]

In view of this wave of persecution, the extensive emigration in 1549 and the following years (until 1553) can no longer be called an inexplicable phenomenon, but only the normal result of the severe action of the government against the followers of the Reformation in the Southern Netherlands. The fact that this ruthless persecution broke out everywhere about 1550 is closely connected both with the extension of the inquisitional forces and with the redoubled application of the edicts. The problem of the inquisition in the Netherlands, especially in the South, and the applications of the complex of edicts, have been given an excellent treatment by the Catholic historian J. Scheerder, who made a praiseworthy attempt to avoid the bias of the deplorable polemically slanted works.[31] Besides synthesizing the known facts, he has gathered numerous new data which we shall use occasionally.

28 Van Braght, *Mirror*, II, p. 139.
29 *B.R.N.*, II, p. 241.
30 P. Génard, *AA*, VIII, p. 469.
31 Joseph Scheerder, *De inquisitie in de Nederlanden in de XVIe eeuw* (Antwerp, 1944).

After Frans van der Hulst, appointed inquisitor on April 23, 1522, had been dismissed from office because of falsification of documents, Oliver Buedens, provost at St. Maartens in Ypres, Nikolaas Houzeau van Bergen, and Jan Coppin, dean of St. Pieters in Louvain, were appointed as general inquisitors. After Coppin's death the pope appointed two other clergymen as general inquisitors: Ruard Tapper from Enkhuyzen, dean of St. Pieters in Louvain, and Michiel Driutius, official of the bishop of Liége at Louvain. On order of Charles V these ecclesiastical dignitaries used their right to appoint assistants in the provinces in 1545. Thus there came to Flanders Pieter Titelman, Dean of Ronse, and Jan Pollet, canon of St. Pieters at Rijsel. They were charged with the purging of the province of all heretical activity. Especially Titelman and his attorney Nicolaas de Hondt, who was in charge of taking notes and keeping record of the accumulating information, became notorious as inquisitors.

Titelman considered it useless to combat the Reformation by trying to convert the heretics with religious discussions and disputes. His strategy allowed only one means to make a final purification; namely, brutal extermination. To reach this goal all the forces of church and state had to co-operate. When Titelman attempted to execute this program in utmost thoroughness in Flanders, his work was undermined by the refusal of the city governments, which felt their ancient prerogatives threatened by the stubborn resistance of the menaced Protestant groups, and also by the disgust of the populace, whose interests were poorly served by the ever-increasing emigration.

An anonymous manifesto from Hondschoote, probably inspired by returning emigrants, argued in 1561, for the first time in print, that the work of Titelman and his helpers would drive prosperity from the town. For that matter, it had by now become well known that the establishment of the Inquisition together with the resultant emigration had caused a serious decline in the national industrial level. Discontent mounted when this economic disorder was accompanied by a rise in prices, the price of wheat, for instance, doubling within one year (1565-66). The attitude of the people toward the clergy did not improve. To their great surprise the churchgoers in Bruges found a manifesto on their church doors in the middle of October, 1564, which seriously criticized certain clergymen.

The inquisitor and his delegates had still more to endure. At Belle, Andries Futtemael threw a pole between the legs of the horse on which Nicolaas de Hondt was riding on the way to have Mahieu Quilz brought to the prison in Ypres.[32] In Ghent, Joos van der Meere and Lysbette

<hr />

32 Ghent State, *RVSC*, 1558-62, fol. 230vof.

Biericx declared that in 1557 they saw some unknown person with a drawn knife attack the same Nicolaas de Hondt, as he was about to arrest Hermes Slosse, saying: "You shall not arrest him; you are not an authorized officer."[33] These last words are typical; they reveal the tension between the ecclesiastical and secular authorities concerning the means of fighting the Reformation.

Since 1545 Titelman had moved heaven and earth to extend his hegemony over all administrative bodies, ecclesiastical as well as civil, and to dedicate everything to the project dearest to him; namely, the extinction of the heretics. While in Brabant the resistance of the civil authorities immediately became so substantial that after 1529 no eccelsiastical inquisitor could summon a lay person for heresy, the final reaction in Flanders did not take place until the second half of the sixteenth century. The cause of this reaction was unquestionably Titelman's excesses.[34] It soon became impossible for him to carry out his program in the Flemish regions where the Reformation had penetrated deeply. For instance, the authorities remained passive when the inquisitor was prevented by crowds of two or three hundred from making a planned arrest.[35] The resistance of the municipal authorities expressed itself also in delaying action when they were to hold trials or to pronounce and execute sentences.[36]

At Ghent the government held the Mennonites Mynkin le Duc and Tannekin Gressy imprisoned for over a year, making no move toward execution in spite of the unshakable determination of the prisoners to adhere to their faith.[37] Of eleven Mennonites turned over by Titelman to the same government in January and April, 1561, not one had been

---

33 Ghent City, *Crime*, 1555-61, fol. 34-35vo. Another equally representative incident took place in June, 1564. During the transport of Daniel du Bois from Ghent to Zeeland, where he was to go to the gallows, the guard was attacked by three or four hundred men. From all sides the crowd shouted at the guards that they, and not the convict, belonged on the gallows. Succumbing to superior numbers, the soldiers withdrew to the prison. (Louis Prosper Gachard, *Correspondance de Philippe II* [Brussels, 1848-1936], II, p. 509.)

34 In his defense Titelman held to the following theses: (1) The institution of the Inquisition endows it with privileges; its activities should not be thwarted. (2) The Inquisition is an ecclesiastical court; within its jurisdiction it should be able to count on the support of all civil authorities. (3) Heresy is a threat to both church and state. (4) The king has always urged his subjects to support the Inquisition. (5) During his thirteen years in the office of inquisitor, there were no complaints; if there are any now, they are to be attributed to heretical influences. (6) He did not infringe on any of the cities' privileges. (7) The greatest evil is the uncontrolled residence of foreigners in the cities. (Victor Gaillard, *Archives du Conseil de Flandre* [Ghent, 1856], pp. 195-98.)

35 Gaillard, *op. cit.*, p. 204.

36 Passchier de Valckenaere, bailiff of Noortberkin, had to pay a large fine and to submit to a public act of humiliation in 1564 because of his feeble prosecution of heretics.

37 Gachard, *Correspondance*, II, pp. 479 f.

sentenced by the end of June.[38] The chief bailiff of Ghent went even farther. When five prisoners, among them one Mennonite, Mattheys, escaped from prison on June 2, 1560, he does not seem to have taken the matter too seriously, for on June 15 Margaret of Parma expressed her displeasure at finding that the negligent jailer was still in office.[39]

In the jurisdictional territory of Ghent, Titelman was also hindered by administrative entanglements. In 1562 and again in 1564 he became the victim of the sharp rivalry between the chief bailiff of Ghent and the neighboring bailiff of den Oudburg. On January 7, 1562, the inquisitor complained to the Council of Flanders that he could not leave Ghent because of the negligent attitude of the bailiffs of Ghent and of den Oudberg, both of whom refused to sentence the three Mennonites whom he, Titelman, held prisoner.[40] A second letter, sent on January 10, 1562,[41] resulted in the Council of Flanders circumventing the quarrel by charging the government of Ghent with the case.[42] A few years later (March, 1564) Titelman once more had to ask the intervention of the Council of Flanders in a similar case.[43] Another typical case of conflict between Titelman and the Flemish cities has been elaborately described by J. Scheerder.[44]

In January, 1562, two manual laborers, Philippe Mallart and Simon Faveau, were arrested in Valenciennes. Though their trial proved them to be persistent heretics, the government was afraid to apply the edicts to them or to execute the sentence, for the Calvinists, who were restless again in the city, threatened the authorities with revenge if they dared to kill the prisoners. On March 22 the rumor was spread that the following night the two prisoners would be executed. In the afternoon two or three hundred masked man could be seen walking on the main market square in groups of six or seven, some of them armed with swords, until they were driven away by rain at about four o'clock. The magistrate postponed the execution on the pretext that there was hope of converting the prisoners. The regent ordered the sentence to be executed, along with

38 Gaillard, *op. cit.*, pp. 206 f.

39 Gachard, *loc. cit.*

40 Ghent City, *Serie 93 bis* reg. M.M., fol. 302vo; *Crime*, 1561-63, pp. 108 f. On p. 108 we find the following note in the margin: "Concerning a certain prisoner about whom there is a jurisdictional conflict between those of Ghent and the bailiff of den Oudburg."

41 Ghent City, *Serie 93 bis,* reg. M.M. fol. 303vo, 304vo; *Crime*, 1561-63, pp. 109 f.; *KR,* 1561-70, fol. 230vo-231vo.

42 *Ibid., Serie 93 bis,* reg. M.M., fol. 304vof.

43 Prudent van Duyse and Edmond de Busscher, *Inventaire analytique des Chartes et documents* . . . (Ghent, 1844-53), Nr. 1.228 (March 24, 1564), p. 429. Some Mennonites had been taken prisoner in the house of de Sceppere in the territory of the Lord of Oomberghe, which was under the jurisdiction of the bailiff of den Oudburg.

44 J. Scheerder, *op. cit.*, pp. 90 ff.

suitable measures to maintain public order. The talk in the taverns threatened violence. At the end of their resources, the magistrate sent a pensioner and an alderman to the regent for new instructions. In the session of the State Council it was proposed that the Margrave of Berghen go to Valenciennes in person to carry out the execution. Displeased by the assignment, he declared that the case was not important enough to take him to Valenciennes; it would be sufficient if he stayed in the vicinity of Mons or Cambrai and this would be known in Valenciennes. In the presence of the regent and the Council of State, he severely reprimanded the two delegates and ordered them to depart immediately.

After the return of the delegates the magistrates let a few more days pass. Finally the execution was set for April 27. The stake was surrounded by an iron fence; measures were taken to bring the prisoners to the place of execution without contact with the people. The guilds and sixty prominent citizens were summoned and armed to suppress possible riot. Under strongly armed guard the prisoners were brought from the dungeon to the stake. Suddenly a group of five or six hundred people, common folk of all ages and both sexes, began to stone the procession. The authorities retreated, fearing that the convicts would escape in the riot. The sectarians knelt and thanked God for this rescue of their fellow believers. Then they tore down the iron fence, scattered the fagots, and set out to loot the Dominican monastery. On their way they changed their minds, however, and stormed the prison and liberated the two fellow believers. They brought them in a procession to the cattle market and there preached a sermon. The magistrate remained passive, merely closing and guarding the city gates; but the citizens in charge of the guard let anyone pass. Mallart and Faveau escaped to England.

These few examples may suffice to show that the municipal governments tended toward passivity, and that this attitude was based on the threat of resistance from the populace.

The chronicler Renon de France went one step further and declared that in the period 1555-62 the city officials themselves were infected by heresy or were at least sympathetic toward the followers of the new faiths. "Most of the officers side with the sectarians and heretics, even with the Anabaptists. Some say that their conscience does not allow them to judge at all, to say nothing of applying the death penalty. Even if a prisoner remains obstinate, a large part of the Council refuses to judge, or at most they send the most stubborn ones to the galleys."[45]

The laxity of the magistrates, whether intentional or not, was not the only cross for Titelman. A stumbling block at least as great for the

---

45 Renon de France, *Histoire des Troubles des Pays-Bas* (Brussels, 1886-91), I, p. 47.

inquisitor was the hopeless indifference of the Council of Flanders, who in this period preferred to avoid direct contact with the difficult problem of the Reformation. When in 1560 Titelman was at his wits' end with Joos de Reux, he finally appealed to the Council to concern itself with the juridical procedure, but received the answer that the gentlemen had no time and that he should deal with the competent commissioners.[46] On May 16, 1561, the inquisitor again complained to the Council, demanding more help in the fulfillment of his duties.[47] His voice was unheard as that of one crying in the wilderness.

Titelman's work in the Flemish towns and villages was becoming increasingly difficult, so much so that even his life was often in danger during his attacks on heretical groups. In his letter to Margaret of Parma (October 27, 1561) he asked her to provide him with a permanent body-guard of six soldiers to enable him to exercise his office of inquisitor under safer and more normal conditions.[48] The regent was too well aware of the tension between the clerical investigators and the cities, proud of their privileges, to enrage the latter still more by granting Titelman these soldiers; consequently her answer of November 1, 1561, was unequivocally negative.[49] Only a few weeks later the inquisitor renewed his request before the Council of Flanders, but this time his proposal found even less hearing. His position became still more hazardous in 1563, when the Antwerp government, thanks to the strong and shrewd leadership of Jacob van Wesenbeke, achieved a great victory over the ecclesiastical authorities: neither Inquisition nor bishop was to have any judicial status. Undoubtedly this victory over the royal will encouraged other cities to protest, even in Flanders where the chastisement of Ghent for the 1540 revolt must certainly have still been fresh in everyone's memory.

In 1564 the bomb burst: Bruges, Ghent, Ypres, and Bruges' Free-land stepped determinedly out of the shadow of passive resistance and joined forces in the effort to destroy Titelman's hegemony. In their request of October 20 to Margaret of Parma they pilloried in sharp words the inquisitor's intolerable arbitrariness and disregard of their ancient privileges.[50] The basic charge was that Titelman had gone so far as to enter homes and arrest citizens without previously informing the

---

46 Ghent State, *RVSC*, 1558-62, fol. 148vof.

47 Gaillard, *op. cit.*, p. 204. In this letter Titelman declares, "My Lords, it is high time to take steps to avoid disaster; if I do not receive assistance I declare myself innocent before God and before the king when I see my efforts fruitless for want of assistance."

48 Gaillard, *op. cit.*, p. 224 f.

49 *Ibid.*, p. 226.

50 L. P. Gachard, *Correspondance de Marguerite d'Autriche avec Philippe II* (Brussels, 1867-81), III, p. 417.

magistrate. Alarmed by the growing resistance—the four allies of Flanders sent three more requests—they urged the inquisitor to be more moderate and discreet than he had been in the last few months. They proposed to Philip II, besides modification of the edicts and of the Inquisition, that he give Titelman the title of "judge ecclesiastique"[51] since "inquisiteur" had become so unpopular. But the Spanish king, Philip II, blinded by his religious fanaticism, would hear of no compromise. The meeting of the Council of State in December, 1564, as well as a meeting of bishops, theologians, and magistrates in May and early June, 1565, were overruled by his unshakable will. In his famous letters from Segovia he left no room for the slightest misunderstanding: both the edicts and the Inquisition were to be maintained in full force.[52]

Hardly had Margaret of Parma, after delaying a whole week, publicized these documents, when a storm of protest arose throughout the Netherlands against which she was absolutely powerless.

The Iconoclasm and the first rumors of war were on their way, dreadful heralds of a long-lasting period of uninterrupted religious and political tension.

In this period of increasing administrative confusion and of active resistance among the people, the Reformation spread in the province as never before. Indisputably the feeble action of the magistrates, undercutting the work of the heretic-hunter Titelman, made the already fearless preachers still more daring. Not only did Calvinism, during the period 1550-66, get its roots deep into the broadest strata of society; not only was Lutheranism rejoicing in a remarkable growth in Bruges and Antwerp; Mennonitism at this time also wrote some of the most heroic pages of its history on Flemish soil.

After the Mennonite brotherhood had had to fight a severe battle just after the mid-century, with the forces of magistrates and inquisitors temporarily uniting, its followers had taken up with unbroken zeal the difficult work of reconstruction. The synchronized attacks made throughout the country in 1551, which resulted in sharper control in the next few years,[53] had thoroughly shaken the Mennonite congregations. Many brethren had left their homeland for the Northern Netherlands, England, or Germany.

---

51 P. Frédéricq. *Trav. pratiques,* II, p. 126. The term is cited by E. Hubert in his introduction to the "Table chronologique du registre sur le faict des Hérésies et Inquisition."

52 J. Scheerder, *op. cit.,* pp. 92-94.

53 A typical case is recorded for August, 1558, in Courtrai, where a father, himself a faithful Catholic, was condemned to public penitence because he had given lodging to his own son "even though he knew that he had been rebaptized" (Courtrai City, *Crimineele procéduren,* 1552-61, fol. 145).

Yet we should be careful not to exaggerate. Many a Mennonite left the town he knew best, but before resorting to a long journey to distant places tried to settle in one of the large Flemish cities. A study of the martyrs' lists, already compiled, gives ample confirmation of this. The Courtrai martyrology shows that the Mennonites who were executed in this city from 1552 to 1569 came from the most varied districts: Lendelede, Halewyn, Deinze, Gullegem, Rekkem, Langemark, Rijsel, Neder-Waasten, Lauwe, Komen, and Zwevegem. The Ghent martyrs' list shows a still wider diversity in towns of origin. Among the Mennonites executed from 1552 to 1569 there were people from other Flemish big cities and even some from the North. We find mentioned Wervik, Louvain, Courtrai, Komen, Brussels, Leiden, Lier, Meenen, Ondersele (near Cassel), Waasten, Nukerke, Belle, Poperinge, Bruges, Oudenaarde, Hamme (near Dendermonde), Maren (near 's Hertogenbosch), Merendree, Landegem, Zandbergen, Moerbek (near Geeraardsbergen), Lokerhoute, Nevele, Deinze, Hansbeke, Deventer, Bassey (Artesie), Tielt, and Evergem. A look at the Bruges martyrology for the period 1558-69[54] shows the following list of towns: Nukerke, Ghent, Sluis, Komen, Middelburg (Zeeland), Zwevezele, Wincle, Diksmuide, Hondschoote, Sint-Winnoxbergen, Cassel, Bellegem (Courtrai), Zwevegem, Leisele (Veurne), Courtrai, and Ypres.

That the emigration to foreign countries took on large proportions cannot be doubted. Yet, as the martyrologies show, an important number of the hunted Mennonites remained in the country and joined the brotherhoods in other cities in the hope—alas, too often vain—of escaping the searchlight of the investigator.[55] Consequently the life of many Men-

---

54 Cf. Verheyden, *Bruges*, under the dates indicated. The date 1569 marks a new period of systematic persecution and brings a new disorganization into the Mennonite fold. The periods covered by these three lists vary because they include only death sentences pronounced against Mennonites. The first victims of the second half of the century fell at Ghent in 1552, at Courtrai in 1553, and at Bruges in 1558.

55 Antwerp was generally thought to be one of the best places of refuge for those who would not leave the Southern Netherlands. The authorities were aware of this. Adrien Vanneaulx, who was suspected of Mennonite activity, had succeeded in escaping the death penalty. But since it was doubted whether he would in the future behave as a good Catholic, it was proposed to Philip II that he be obliged to live permanently in Douai or Tournai. As for Antwerp, this city hardly could be considered, since "he could very well keep hidden and relapse into said sect and company."

Nevertheless many were trapped in the capital. The promise of rewards for betrayal of teachers (who presumably had close contact with the Antwerp brotherhood) was seldom successful, but some members were actually caught and arrested. This was the fate of Barbara and Medara Catz of Wervik, Symon Dondt of Ghent, Joos van Beke of Dentegem, Jan Poote from near Hasselt, who had joined the brotherhood in 1552 or 1553, Hans and Gheert Vermandele of Courtrai, Jaques Semou of Bethune, Peeter Verlomgen of Courtrai, Guillaume de Clerck of Meenen, Baltazar de Rosières of Tournai, Jan Ghyselinck of Bruges (the church's

nonites became a hard wanderer's existence; a new place of residence had to give not only some guarantee of "safety," but also an opportunity for the fugitive to find work in order to keep his family alive.

Besides furnishing clear proof for the movements of the brethren within the boundaries of Flanders these enumerations also give a substantial view of the expansion of Mennonitism. They prove primarily that the brotherhoods survived the disconcerting blow of 1551 and continued as an important religious movement. The most important result was that the Mennonite groups—contrary to what has usually been said by Southern Netherlands historians—by no means receded into the background during the second half of the sixteenth century. This fact is of primary importance, considering the imminent Iconoclasm, because their absolute neutrality in this outburst of violence cannot possibly be attributed to numerical weakness.

The problem of the significance of the Mennonite expansion in the pre-Iconoclasm period is too important to be passed over lightly here. It will, of course, be impossible to present exact figures for the size of the Mennonite groups, since the documents are silent on this matter, and we therefore need to be satisfied with what the archival materials reveal about the number of meetings held and the evidence they offer about Mennonites living in certain centers.

The picture of the expansion of Mennonitism before 1566 acquired from the study of the archives must be regarded as incomplete, except in the case of the large cities. Indeed, every large Flemish city was continually host to zealous propagandists of Menno's teachings, not excluding extremely conservative Bruges. This fact is supported by certain archival materials, here examined in chronological order, which not only reveal constant Mennonite preaching in the cities, but also throw light on the spread of Mennonite teachings in the rural areas.

It is peculiar that, except for the loss of Jan Helleman (burned at the stake on January 16, 1552), the brotherhood in Bruges suffered no persecution after 1551.[56] Although Pauwels Vermaete[57] had held meetings in the city regularly since 1548, it was not until 1552 that the magistrate was informed of the fact. It certainly is a testimonial to the reputation of the brethren involved and also to the solid organization of their congregation that the city authorities could arrest no one in spite of their knowledge of the meetings.

---

messenger who informed the faithful when and where meetings were to be held), Jan de Tymmerman of Courtrai, Mayken Christiaens of Nijpkerke, Jan van Akeren of Courtrai, Jan van de Walle of Eeke, and Calleken Meeuwels of Courtrai. (Génard, *op. cit.*, II, p. 375; XII, pp. 336-63; XIII, pp. 12-29, 33-38.)

56 Verheyden, *Bruges*, p. 36.   57 *Ibid.*, p. 45.

In Ghent the arrests and executions of Mennonites in 1551 did not interrupt the congregational life. In the period 1552-53 many meetings were held and several baptismal ceremonies performed with the assistance of Cornelis Claissone from Leiden,[58] Jan van de Walle,[59] and a certain Christiaen.[60] Their activity was very effective, as shown by the testimonies of 1555, which give us the picture of a thriving congregation.

Adrien Vanneaulx, of Douai, related that during his journeys he repeatedly had opportunity to listen to Mennonite teaching in the East Flemish capital (he also admitted having attended meetings in Tournai). In 1555 the wedding of Jerosme van der Cappellen with Margriet Vanneaulx was performed here.[61] In the meantime other powerful leaders had arisen in the group at Ghent, Pieter Coerte, Antheunis Hellegoete, Hans de Vette, Caerle Tanghereet, and Adriaen Petersz-Pan, all of whom paid for their zeal with their lives.[62]

On July 31, 1561, Tannekin Telmeere testified to Titelman and Pieter de Backere that she had left the Catholic Church in 1550. She had then regularly attended the Mennonite meetings and had finally been baptized in 1560 at Ghent by "Joos" (this was all she would say).[63] Martin Micron, the violent opponent of the Mennonites, had to admit that they had a powerful influence in the Southern Netherlands in 1555.[64] From 1555 on, interesting data about the spread of Menno's teachings also reaches us from outside the foci of Ghent and Bruges. The author of the Doopsgezinde martyrology, Thieleman van Braght, tells of a rich cloth merchant, Lenaert Plovier, who publicly joined the local brotherhood at Meenen.[65]

Again it is certain that Jacques de Rore led the first meeting at Roeselaere in 1556,[66] while one year afterward the presence of Joachim

58 Verheyden, Ghent, p. 18.
59 Verheyden, Bruges, p. 46.
60 Ghent State, RVSF, Nr. 21.
61 Brussels Royal, EA, 1177/1 and 1177/3.
62 Verheyden, Ghent, p. 25. Adriaen Petersz Pan was beheaded at Antwerp on June 18, 1559. Probably he was a teacher at Ghent. If not, he had at least been working in the church there and knew it well, as his letter to the brotherhood in the city testifies. (B.R.N., II pp. 373-92; Vos, DtA, pp. 360 f.)
63 Ghent City, Crimineel Sententieboek, 1561-65, p. 30. Tanneken Delmeere was arrested with Lynken Claes; both remained true to their faith. After the authorities had attempted repeatedly to convert them, the two women asked the jailer to go to the presiding councilman to inform him that further efforts would be fully useless. (Ibid., p. 32.)
64 Vos, DtA, p. 328.
65 Van Braght, Mirror, II, pp. 270 f. Jooris Wippe, who was also converted, was however not the burgomaster of Meenen, as van Braght (II, p. 203) reports (communication from Mr. Krahé).
66 Verheyden, Bruges, pp. 58-60.

Vermeeren is reported at Meenen.[67] A very interesting glimpse of the spread of Mennonitism in Flanders before 1558 is provided by the trial documents of the Mennonites executed in that year in Bruges.[68] Jacob de Zwarte from Nukerke had for some time been in sympathy with the Mennonites in Oostende and Hondschoote; in the latter town he was baptized in 1557. For unknown reasons (was he already suspected?) he left this town and settled in Bruges early in 1558. Here he gave his full support to the proclamation of Menno's teachings, which cost him his life at the stake on August 15, 1558.

In the midst of the brotherhood of Bruges, Jacob de Zwarte had learned to know Jan Vervest, a zealous Mennonite propagandist, a former actor of Ghent, who had been in the Mennonite movement for many years. Acquainted with the Mennonites in the city of his birth before 1551, he belonged to the refugee group mentioned in the Memoire-Book of Ghent. Too well known in Flanders, he planned to settle in some Northern Netherlands town. Neither at Amsterdam nor at Dordrecht did he succeed satisfactorily in finding work to make a living for his large family (he had three sons and two daughters.) Finally he risked once more going to Ghent. He endangered his life further by openly joining the Mennonites shortly after his return and being baptized by Gillis van Aken. But when the inquisitors made a new attack on the Ghent congregation, he fortunately escaped once more. Realizing the uselessness of another trip to the North, he settled in Bruges, where he was employed by Frans Dhondt.

From now on Jan Vervest dedicated himself completely to the spreading of Mennonitism in Bruges, faithfully supported by his wife, Livine Verwee, who had been baptized at Ghent in 1555 by Gillis van Aken, and who matched her husband in zeal in defending the faith. In their home many meetings were held, where experienced Mennonites contributed their support to the strengthening of the foundations of the Bruges brotherhood. Among the faithful attendants was sixty-year-old Pauwels Vermaete of Sluis, a convert of Jan van Tricht, who had been in the Mennonite movement since 1537. In the meetings at Jan Vervest's home he was the minister; so it is not strange that when he was arrested in 1558 he was carrying a New Testament, an edition of the Psalms, and a martyr book. He also led other meetings at the home of the emigrant Marten van de Walle from Ghent, who was so openly Mennonite after his baptism by Gillis van Aken, that when the persecution broke out in 1551 he felt unsafe in his birthplace. After wandering for many years, he

---

67 Vos, *DtA*, p. 343.
68 Verheyden, *Bruges*, pp. 41-47.

finally settled at Bruges in 1557. It is not impossible that his younger brother, Jan van de Walle, "teacher" in the Antwerp congregation, visited him at Bruges and was active there.

In the same group of prominent Mennonites in Bruges who became martyrs in 1558 were also Jan de la Beecke of Komen, and Vervest's cousin, Hans van den Broucke of Ghent. All the meetings were announced to the brethren by Franchois van Ieper, who was never captured.

The trials of these Mennonites reveal great activity prior to 1558 in Hondschoote, Meenen, Vladsloo, Werken, Wervik, Poperinge, and Gistel. According to the statements of Calleken Vermaete, the eighteen-year-old daughter of Pauwels Vermaete, Gistel was not very suitable for large meetings. It is nevertheless remarkable that she and her father went to Gistel, of all places, to hide from the investigators. It should also be remembered that Pauwels Vermaete as Mennonite "teacher" was especially hunted. Without the existence of a trustworthy group his staying at Gistel as a noncitizen would, in our opinion, have been impossible. It is thus very probable that from the second half of the sixteenth century there was in this town a Mennonite nucleus which, however, could not risk holding meetings on a large scale but rather limited its activities to strictly closed meetings.

That Mennonitism in this period reached one of its high points of expansion is most evident from Titelman's own testimonies. The regent, Margaret of Parma, received a letter from him dated October 17, 1561, in which he declared: "I find this sect to be increasing in several places."[69] His next letter, dated November 14, 1561,[70] sounded even more desperate: it was a settled matter for him that Flanders was completely infected by Menno's teachings. During his trips he had discovered that at Ypres, Poperinge, Meenen, Armentières, Hondschoote, and Antwerp extensive congregations were enjoying an unheard-of prosperity. In the first two towns he had succeeded (so he claimed) in destroying the groups though, as he had to admit, many members had escaped him and fled. Concerning Armentières he reports that the celebration of the Lord's Supper had to be repeated three times because of the large size of the congregation; each time the ceremony was attended by eighty or one hundred persons. In Antwerp the situation was still more critical: here the teachers had to circulate among twenty-five or thirty meetings in order to give all members the opportunity to partake in the ceremony.

There actually is a climax in this letter. Titelman made no attempt

69 Gaillard, *op. cit.*, p. 224.

70 *Ibid.*, pp. 230-32; de Coussemaker, *Troubles*, I, pp. 86-88; Gachard, *Correspondance de Philippe II*, II, p. 484.

to go into detail on Hondschoote and was content to state: "As for Hondschoote, there is no number to be given; it is a bottomless abyss."[71] In a later writing (1562) he added to this list the cities of Courtrai and Ghent, where he had seized twenty Mennonites.[72] Ghent especially was not in the best of standing in the Brussels government circles. Was it not under Titelman's influence that Margaret of Parma wrote on July 31, 1562, that "at Ghent there are two kinds, Anabaptists and Calvinists"?[73]

The Secret Council sent the Council of Flanders a letter on November 4, 1561, urging it to repress the Reformation more actively and in particular to exterminate the Mennonites. The Secret Council declared, "We understand that the number of Anabaptists increases daily in said country [Flanders]."[74] In the light of this statement it would be impossible to consider as complete the enumeration of Mennonite centers found in Titelman's letters. For that matter, the chief inquisitor himself admitted that he had not had time or opportunity to work out his plans completely or to reach every town.[75] For example, he does not mention Bruges at all, where, without his intervention, twenty-five persons—the great majority of them Mennonites—were arrested in the same year.[76]

The best proof for the growth of the congregation at Bruges is given by Friar Cornelis, who reported that meetings were announced throughout the city. When notoriety and the success of the Anabaptist preaching became too great, the magistrate decided to send a troop of 200 soldiers to stop it. The expedition must not have had the desired results, however, since nothing more is said about arrests or further restrictive measures.[77]

71 In this period the following Mennonites were executed in Hondschoote: Jacop Pierin, Aernoul Herveloo (April 23, 1559); Charles du Vivier (March 9, 1562); Peronne Pertrys (October 3, 1562); Claise Pertrys (October 15, 1562); cf. de Coussemaker, *Troubles*, IV, pp. 135-40. The Hondschoote city financial accounts yield in addition the names of the following martyrs: Frans de Zwaerte, Martincke Aelmaers, Casper Deken, Charles van de Velde (*Ibid.*, IV, p. 283.)

72 De Coussemaker, *Troubles*, I, p. 87. Courtrai had already been investigated by Titelman in 1553. He had then declared, "Nowhere have city and citizens been found to be infected more grossly and with more evil heresies than here" (Courtrai City, *Register van Consultaciën*, fol. 21vo-22).

73 Baron de Reiffenberg, *Correspondance de Marguerite d'Autriche* (Brussels, 1842), p. 127.

74 Brussels Royal, *EA*, 1177/3.

75 De Coussemaker, *op. cit.*, I, p. 87.

76 Stadsarchiv Bruges, Secret resolution of November 26, 1561; Chanoine A. A. de Schrevel, *Histoire du Séminaire de Bruges* (Bruges, 1883), I, p. 691, note 2. In a later writing addressed to Philip on September 27, 1564, Titelman does mention Bruges. Without mentioning the Mennonites specifically, he describes the city as especially infested by heresy (*ubi magna quoque est infectio*). (Gachard, *Correspondance de Marguerite*, III, p. 417.)

77 *Broer Cornelis*, fol. 83vo.

That in Ghent the situation was critical some weeks before the Iconoclasm is attested by the experience of Thomas Streck with the authorities. This eighteen-year-old from Wachtebeke, "very eloquent and able to seduce others," was arrested on February 15, 1566. In spite of repeated efforts by several theologians, he remained true to his Mennonite faith. As could be expected, he was condemned to death in April. However, nothing was done to execute the sentence; the executioner seemed unable to find time or appetite to erect the stake! Shortly afterward (April 9) the Council of Flanders received Margaret's letter urging all governmental agencies to moderate their restrictions on non-Catholic activity. On June 10, 1566, the Council presented the Thomas Streck case to the regent and declared themselves in favor of condemning him to the galleys. In her answer of June 16, Margaret left it to the Council of Flanders to deal with him as they wished. In the meantime, Thomas Streck had learned that his case had taken a favorable turn. The prison walls had not been able to prevent him from hearing news of the increasing power of the non-Catholic part of the population. Very probably this was the reason why he did not cease to ask to be released.[78] He was probably among the Mennonites released on July 24, according to Vaernewijck, to prevent a popular revolt.[79] Only extreme confusion can account for such laxness on the part of the authorities. The fact that a Mennonite was able to evade his sentence proves that Mennonitism had also begun to enjoy a certain liberty during the restless weeks before the Iconoclasm.

Likewise in Southern Flanders the prestige of Mennonitism increased even more, for this area lay between the two radiating centers, Ghent and the northern cities of today's French Flanders (such as Armentières).[80] Furthermore, several particularly zealous preachers counted Southern

78 Brussels Royal, *EA*, Nr. 244/1, items 35 and 36.

79 The Ghent chronicle of Cornelis van Campene speaks of an amnesty for Mennonites in all Flanders, a report which is confirmed by van Vaernewijck for Ghent. In Bruges the report spread that Ghent had released several heretics on July 24, 1566. Immediately the doors of all the churches in Bruges were decorated with a placard in which the same measure was demanded for local prisoners without regard for confession. Bevere, president of the Council of Flanders, explained that those who had been released without further punishment had previously recanted of their heresies. This version of the events is, however, in contradiction to the explicit statement of van Vaernewijck's chronicle, which reports that many Mennonites, including "one teacher with a limp," had been released without even having to pay the costs of their trial. It was difficult for the authorities to get one woman out of prison. She declared, "My dear husband has been killed for the Lord's sake, and all our goods have been taken away; on what shall I, a poor woman, live?" To comfort her she was released without having to pay even the costs of her trial or imprisonment. (Brussels Royal Library, MS 6,336, fol. 7; M. van Vaernewijck, *op. cit.*, I, p. 34; A. C. de Schrevel, *op. cit.*, V, pp. 174 f.; Brussels Royal, *EA, Etat et Audience*, reg. 512; fol. 33, 38.)

80 Cf. the report already mentioned (note 70) which tells of the celebration of communion in three successive gatherings of from 80 to 100 members each.

Flanders as their field of labor. We meet here Jacques de Rore, who was mentioned earlier,[81] and the very capable and eloquent Daniel Vaercampt.[82] Southern Flanders was also the special field of Pauwels van Meenen, who, except for his ministry in Bruges at the home of Maillaert de Grave, was there constantly.[83]

Margaret of Parma learned that Jan Moyaert and Jehan Toullet were influential Mennonite preachers in several towns of Flanders. Since she also had heard that they were hiding in Antwerp, she ordered the margrave, on December 25, 1564, to make a thorough investigation: his report confirmed the facts given by the regent.[84] Abel de Grave admitted to his inquisitors at Bruges that he had attended meetings at Roeselaere and Vladsloo several times.[85]

A synthesis of all this information concerning the spread of the Mennonite teachings is provided by the following passage from a letter by the regent to Count Egmont on January 23, 1565, dealing with the situation in Flanders: "There are sections where the Anabaptists have multiplied greatly."[86] In view of this spread of Mennonite teachings throughout the country it would be indefensible for historians to deny any longer to Mennonitism an important place in the framework of Flemish Reformation life in the period preceding the Iconoclasm. Besides, it is not to be overlooked that the Iconoclasm, as an outburst of a long-restrained desire for practical realization of goals which had been much discussed but never achieved, lay in the line of the aspirations of Menno's followers as much as in those of the Lutherans and Calvinists.

One should not eliminate any of these religious movements from the analysis of the iconoclastic uprising on the ground that it had only a small following: the numerically weaker groups could have seen in a bold outburst the means to achieve more freedom of action, which would then permit unhampered expansion. If one should insist on taking the

81 Verheyden, *Bruges*, p. 59.

82 *Ibid.*

83 *Ibid.*, p. 55.

84 The following details were reported to Margaret of Parma by the margrave on January 9, 1565: "I made all possible haste to obtain information about said two men. I found a Jehan de Moyart, a man of about forty years, of medium stature, small blond beard, married with no children, doing fairly good business with products of Lille and Tournai, living on the market square of this city; have been informed that he is of good reputation. And as for Jehan Toullet of Armentières, I have been told that he is a man of medium stature, stocky, with a black beard beginning to turn gray, and is for the moment in Frankfurt, as he always visits the fairs in that city; and that a few days ago it was further reported that he also visits openly those of Armentières and Bruges" (Gachard, *Correspondance de Marguerite*, III, pp. 536 f.).

85 Bruges State, *Crim. Bouck*, 1561-69, fol. 163vof.

86 Gachard, *Correspondance de Marguerite*, III, p. 545.

factor of numerical strength as a ground for disregarding one of the religious groups in the study of the Iconoclasm, this would have to be Lutheranism, not Mennonitism. The course of events demonstrated, however, that such a standard would lead to wrong conclusions: it has actually been proved that the numerically inferior Lutherans were active in the Iconoclasm.[87]

As for the Mennonites, they were more than ever true to their non-violent principles. The numerous trials, correspondence, and the arguments of justification presented by magistrates who were called to account, all prove this. Nowhere could a Mennonite be brought before the judges on the charge of Iconoclasm. Nowhere had the Mennonites preached sermons of a revolutionary character. Neither the appointed leaders nor the few free-lancing individualists had fallen prey to the temptation to enforce their will by deeds when words did not seem to reach the goal.[88]

In contrast with Lutheranism and Calvinism, Mennonitism, as was said before, resolutely remained aloof from any attempt to conquer the world by violence. Nor were the Mennonites interested in the establishment of an ecclesiastical system which soon would overshadow the Catholic institution. With Menno they wished to establish on this earth their "church of Christ," to which they invited everyone who would leave every worldly ideal behind to devote himself exclusively to the practice of the faith which would prepare him to enter God's kingdom.[89] By the symbol of baptism such persons were adopted into the broad communion of brethren among whom temporal and material things had lost out to the eternal and spiritual realities.

Typical here is the testimony of Hans Vermeersch (executed at Waasten in 1559) who, to the question which was the "true church," quietly and simply answered the inquisitors, "The assembly of believers in Christ's name."[90] This attitude by no means led to a complete isolation from society, but it did commit the Mennonites to strictness and holy

87 J. van Vloten, *Nederlands Tijdens den Volksopstand tegen Spanje* (Schiedam, 1872), p. 83.

88 On May 17, 1567, Pieter de Vynck appeared before the Bruges Council to answer for his attendance at Mennonite meetings and his distribution of Mennonite literature. He was further charged with participating in the Iconoclasm, but he emphatically denied "ever having done such a thing; but at work he saw a statue being broken out of a niche before the cloister, not knowing who did it" (Bruges State, *Crim. Bouck,* 1561-69, fol. 164vo).

89 The testimony of Pieter de Joncheere on December 5, 1561, is a good illustration of this conviction. He once had said that the New Jerusalem was near. Suspected of the worst intentions, he was asked during his trial what he had meant. He answered immediately that he had not been speaking about an earthly but about a heavenly Jerusalem. That he did not say this just to buy his freedom is evident from the consistency of his defense of other Mennonite beliefs. Pieter de Joncheere went to the stake on March 12, 1562. (Ghent City, *Crime,* 1561-63, pp. 97 f.; Verheyden, *Ghent,* p. 27.)

90 Van Braght, *Mirror,* II, p. 260.

living as examples to the sinful world. It was not at all an easily maintained discipline behind cloister walls, but an unshakable self-discipline in the midst of the turbulent atmosphere of the everyday life with its numerous temptations. An attitude of that kind ultimately had to capture the attention of outsiders. Josse de Groote declared in 1566 that he had joined the Mennonites because he "saw too well that of all the new confessions the Mennonite one was the most sincere and maintained a strict discipline."[91]

The voluntary adhesion to the nonresistant position cannot then be called a myth. There is no other explanation for the fact that Mennonites maintained unitedly to the very end their aloofness from the Iconoclasm, than that this aloofness sprang from principle and from their view of the church. To the believer only God's Word was valid as a means of bringing the world to better insights; therefore any means which were not in line with the Gospel were regarded as evil. Their neutrality toward the Iconoclasm was only a normal manifestation of this mentality. It would be wrong to regard this aloofness as arising only when the impending outbreak of violence appeared and for the purpose of distinguishing themselves from some of the leaders of other groups, or to thwart the plans of their Reformed opponents to blame them. What was planned in the Mennonite groups in August, 1566, was not at all new, but only one more proof of the position of complete repudiation of violence which had been completed among them around 1540 in socially restless Flanders. As has already been pointed out, state and church made every possible attempt to prevent the public from learning of the nonresistance of the Mennonites, using posters, sermons, and other theological writings to label this rejection of violence as a clever move to deceive the credulous.[92] This fictitious charge—that the Anabaptists were seeking to win a large following in order to bring about a new revolution which would destroy both religion and social order—was, however, always widely believed.

This accusation was a greater obstacle to the rise of Mennonitism than any persecution. Constantly the Mennonites had to encounter it. The Antwerp congregation left a splendid testimony on this matter: it is known beyond question that Menno had several thousand followers in the capital at the time of the uprising; hence the question of whether to join the other groups for this mass movement must have been acute.

---

91 De Coussemaker, *Troubles*, III, p. 155.

92 The clearest example of the current opinion among the Catholics was given by M. Cunerus Petri in *Den Schilt teghen die Wederdoopers* (Louvain, 1568, fol. 6): "For as long as [the Mennonites] think that they are not yet strong enough, they will keep silent; but when they see their hour and opportunity, it will be too late to resist them."

De Navorscher published in 1862 the text of a request of the Antwerp Mennonites addressed to the governor of the city, Prince William of Orange, asking for recognition.[93] They used the opportunity to refute all the accusations brought against them, though they must have known very well that it would be very difficult to convince the prince.[94] Above all, they were accused of always proclaiming their teachings in secret, even in times of greater freedom, as in 1566: "They play secretly at being 'brethren in Christ.' "[95] Little breath need be wasted to deny once again that the Mennonites allowed polygamy. The main point is that Mennonites were so extraordinarily quiet during these times of tension. Outside the city the meetings were held in strictest secrecy, while practically no meetings were held inside the walls.[96] Behind this abnormal quietness,

93 *De Navorscher*, XII (1862), pp. 366-69.

94 The Prince of Orange had repeatedly pressed Margaret of Parma to be severe in the persecution of the Mennonites. The regent, unwilling to apply discriminatory measures against any one particular branch of the Reformation, had refused to follow his counsel. William would not be discouraged, and wrote to Margaret: "Furthermore, Madame, as for the Anabaptists and the Free Spirits, if Your Highness does not find it good, for reasons mentioned in her last letter, to forbid them everywhere, she should authorize me to forbid them in this city, which would, I think, Madame, be a great service to God and His Majesty and Your Highness" (J. van Wesembeeck, *Beschryvinghe can den staet ende voortganck der religie in Nederlant* [Breda, 1616], p. 185). Concerning the difference of opinion between William and Margaret, cf. further, L. P. Gachard, *Correspondance de Guillaume le Taciturne* [Brussels, 1847-66], II, pp. 221, 226, 229, 258, 263, 385; Henri Pirenne, *Histoire de Belgique* (7 vols., 1899-1932), III, p. 334; Hoynck van Papendrecht, *Analecta Belgica* (The Hague, 1943), IV, pp. 55-59. Génard, *AA*, XI, pp. 65, 71 75.

Typical of the attitude of William of Orange was his order to Adam van Berchem to break up a Mennonite meeting on September 21, 1566, two days before the above request was addressed to Margaret. (Robert van Roosbroeck, ed., *Chronijke van Godevaert van Haecht* [Antwerp, 1929-30], I, p. 108.) This policy is related to the first attempts, probably encouraged by the prince, to reach a religious peace. To this end, just as was to happen after 1575, in the Pacification of Ghent and other similar treaties, an understanding was sought between Catholic and Calvinist groups; Mennonitism, considered by both groups as fanatical, did not even come into the picture. Catholic spokesmen, on the other hand, continued to consider all the movements of Reformation origin as belonging to one anti-Catholic bloc. Granvelle also expressed the opinion of Margaret of Parma when he wrote: "But if, as it seems to be planned, we give freedom to everyone to believe whatever he will, not only will we thenceforth have Catholics and Huguenots together, following the dangerous example of what we have recently seen in France, but also all kinds of Anabaptists" (Gachard, *Correspondance de Philippe II*, III, No. 172; May 6, 1566).

95 On July 31, 1566, a few days before the Iconoclasm, Margaret referred to this clandestine preaching: "Nevertheless the Anabaptists do not preach in public, but secretly, except in Holland and Zeeland, according to my inquiry" (de Reiffenberg, *Correspondance de Marguerite d'Autriche*, p. 127).

96 It is striking that Philippe d'Auxy, the traitor and spy of Antwerp, who certainly did not like the Mennonites, could say nothing about their activities but that they "preach on Camer Street near the Schuttersput, near the home of a brewer" (Génard, *AA*, IX, p. 406). This lack of detail is even more significant because d'Auxy could give detailed lists of the leading persons in the Calvinist and Lutheran churches. He certainly would have done the

their opponents pretended, were hidden the blackest purposes: no doubt before long a storm would blow over the city, and the Mennonites would use that opportunity to impose their power. To these accusations a clear answer was given: the fact that they had refrained from holding any mass meetings during the last few months was explained by their decision not to increase the prince's difficulties as governor of the city.[97] By their aloofness they intended only to help the city authorities in maintaining order. Yet, the petition goes on, they had been compelled to break their long silence with this proclamation because seekers for truth might unwittingly listen to Menno's opponents, to whom their policy of neutrality seemed sheer hypocrisy. Beyond that, it had become too heavy a burden on their conscience to be unfaithful to God's Word any longer, since this urged them to teach (I Peter 3) and to hold meetings (Hebrews 10).

This reappearance and bid for attention was an unparalleled success; but precisely this success increased their fear that their opponents would take up the campaign of calumny with renewed vigor. To prevent the Prince of Orange, and with him the whole city government, from being misled by this slander, they proposed to appear before the city authorities together with their accusers to clear the case definitely. In anticipation of this confrontation, the authors of the request (very probably the spokesmen of the several Antwerp groups) had thought it necessary to meet in advance the main accusations. First of all, they referred to texts from Ecclesiasticus, Matthew, the epistles to Timothy and Titus and those of Peter, to show why they submitted fully to the decisions made by the secular authorities. Further, their opponents should not be believed when they interpreted the Mennonite refusal to take the oath as a means to escape the obligation of loyalty to the legal authorities and to indulge in all kinds of violence. The Mennonites felt themselves bound—the defense continues—to the commandments of the Scriptures, which forbid any taking of the oath. Matthew 5 and James 5. As for all other doctrinal issues which are summarized in the request,[98] they would be glad to

---

same for the Mennonites, had he had the information. Likewise little was known about the group meeting outside the city, though it was well attended. Margaret declared to William of Orange in a letter of July 25, 1566, that the Mennonites seemed not to want their numerical strength to be known to outsiders. "I have been warned that in a certain house in the new town, opposite the house of the Oisterlins in Antwerp, there are frequently meetings of the Anabaptists, early in the morning, sometimes three or four hundred persons, who meet in several shifts, not all appearing at the same time, thus not showing how many they are, since they know very well they are disliked by all other sects" (Génard, *AA*, X, p. 425).

97 The texts published in Prims' *Wonderjaar* make clear that the situation in Antwerp in 1566 was really threatening.

98 "For we believe everything which the Holy Scriptures testify concerning: God the Father, His Son, His holy Incarnation, His salvation. Furthermore we believe what the Scrip-

defend them before the governor. Finally they argued that the great diversity in confessions cannot be seen as an abnormality, since according to Matthew 10 there can never be unanimity in such matters. They seemed to attach great value to this argument, for by it they hoped to persuade the prince to grant the rights of citizenship to Mennonites. They expected him to issue an order to end the unfair discrimination under which they still suffered ("for we are despised by many and regarded as atrocious").

This request was dated September 13, 1566. Actually it belongs to the post-Iconoclasm period. Yet it still has great value for the insight it affords into typical Mennonite attitudes in these restless weeks. It also provides an indisputable proof that their neutrality was not a diplomatic move but a sincere and spontaneous attitude. This was true not only of the Antwerp Mennonites; throughout the Flemish country they maintained the same neutrality.

It would be hard to deny that their attitude during the Iconoclasm contributed much to bring them into a more favorable light in the eyes of the mass of the people. It is remarkable that their significance, already great before and during the "Wonder Year," becomes actually preponderant in the years immediately following, until the outburst of the new wave of persecution in 1568. The provost Morillon pictured the growth of Mennonitism as terrifying (September 15, 1566).[99]

Certainly the serious damage in the ranks of the Calvinists had something to do with this situation. Except for a few executions of Calvinists, the magistrate did not succeed in catching the most influential propagandists. Most of them had gone abroad to bide their time. The Calvinists who were left behind felt disabled by the absence of their leaders: often they joined the Mennonites.

The Calvinist author Guy de Brès addressed a writing to the Antwerp consistorium on this matter, warning them against the "Anabaptist danger": "I have been greatly grieved about what has been told me, that the Anabaptists are spoiling many of our people; I pray you, my very dear brethren, to look out closely for this evil, that you may keep your hands

tures testify about the true righteousness, God's punishing and wrath on all evil and unrighteousness of men, and about the true repentance and forgiveness of sins for all the converted, etc. Furthermore about the commandment and practice of baptism and its meaning, and the meaning of the Lord's Supper, and of marriage, of the ordination of bishops and deacons, of the evangelical ban or exclusion, of the love for God and the neighbor and all men, of the resurrection from the dead, etc., which would take too long to explain here."

99 Edmond Poullet and Charles Piot, *Correspondance du Cardinal de Granvelle* (Brussels, 1877-96), I, p. 465; "There is also an infinity of Anabaptists, whose sect and doctrine multiplies from day to day."

clean of the blood of those who have been placed under your charge."[100]
His information was correct and his fears well founded.

This growth of the Mennonites, however bad its results may have
been for the Calvinists, was important first of all because it forced the
city authorities to intervene vigorously and immediately. Only a few
weeks after the Iconoclasm the Mennonites held meetings outside the
Peterselie Gate in Ghent, at each of which 300 or more were counted.
During these meetings the speakers not only proclaimed their own teachings, but also attacked the Calvinists and their ministers, whom they pictured to be "rebellious people, seekers for revenge." This is another proof
of their irreproachable behavior; for to express this judgment without
being innocent themselves would have been senseless.

The result of these attacks on the Calvinists was that in September,
1566, two debates were held between a Calvinist minister and a Mennonite spokesman. According to van Vaernewijck, the twenty-year-old Mennonite finally won the debate.[101]

Nor were the Catholics spared by the Mennonite reaction. On September 29 Jan van der Haeghen was interrupted during his sermon in the
St. Jacobs Church by a Mennonite who shouted "that all was evil and
false that he [van der Haeghen] was teaching the people."[102]

All these eloquent evidences of a strongly developing Mennonite
group forced the magistrate to interfere. In the middle of October, 1566,
the Ghent authorities sent an armed band to attack a Mennonite meeting.[103] Although it proved to be a false alarm, the use of soldiers indicated
the possibility that—according to the information received by the city
authorities—a well-attended meeting could be held.

In October, 1567, the magistrate of Meenen took similar precau-
tions.[104] In Courtrai the Mennonites were the only ones to continue the
work of the Reformation, while the Calvinists kept silent for a time.[105]
At Ypres the Mennonites felt so safe that they no longer thought it nec-

---

100 Brussels Royal, *Manuscrits divers*, No. 182, fol. 156. This movement of Calvinists into
the Mennonite fellowship is confirmed by van Vaernewijck, who estimates the number of
known Mennonites at 400. *(Van die beroerlicke tijden, II, p. 335.)*

101 Van Vaernewijck, *op. cit.*, I, p. 241 f.

102 De Jonghe, *Ghent*, I, p. 46.

103 *Ibid.*, p. 49. That the Ghent authorities thus took the initiative in repressing the
Mennonites is surprising, for Ghent had hitherto proclaimed only reluctantly and upon the
special insistence of the Duke of Alva the edict against heresy which the royal government
renewed regularly twice a year from June 24, 1557, to June 23, 1566. (Ghent State, *RVBW*,
reg. 80, fol. 133vo.)

104 Van Vaernewijck, *op. cit.*, III, p. 119. The bailiff failed to capture any Mennonites,
but immediately had all their goods confiscated.

105 Brussels Royal, *EA*, No. 244/2, item 62.

essary to have secret meetings; every meeting was well attended. This South Flemish bulwark of Mennonitism disconcerted the governor Egmont, for he could not give up the idea that there might be violence. For that reason he assigned to a group of twelve soldiers the task of hunting out every meeting of non-Catholic character in the district.[106]

Many meetings were held at Poperinge in the home of Augustyn Gloribus, who escaped the hands of the Inquisition by flight in 1568.[107] Less fortunate was the weaver, Jan Portier, who went to the stake in November of the same year at Meenen.[108] At Winnoxbergen Jan Kerbusch spoke several times to the many fellow believers and even baptized there.[109] At Hondschoote the situation was bad for the government. The informers Pieter le Cocq and Lievin Snouck reported that six or seven thousand people lived apart from the Catholic Church "in several sects,"[110] among which the Mennonites were strongly represented.[111] In this period the Mennonite teachings prospered also around Geeraardsbergen. Several brethren fell into the hands of the court, but escaped from prison with the help of the jailer.[112]

At Bruges Friar Cornelis lamented on February 15, 1568, the weakness of Protestantism in his city and stated that "their devilish congregation [Mennonite] is at least seven hundred strong in this city of Bruges."[113]

In the fold of the Bruges congregation there were many Mennonites from outside the city, fourteen of whom fell into the hands of the authorities in February, 1568.[114] In the area along the coast—at Oostende—Lucas de Groot was hanged as a Mennonite.[115]

During the first years after the Iconoclasm, Mennonitism developed under entirely different conditions. Until then the churches had been compelled by necessity to accept leadership from the North. But, as men-

---

106 Bruges State, *Kastelnij Ieper, Troubles religieux du XVIe siècle:* November 16, 17, 25, 1567.

107 Van Braght, *Mirror,* II, p. 367.

108 Brussels Royal, *EA,* No. 512, fol. 318vo-321.

109 De Coussemaker, *op. cit.,* III, pp. 153 f.

110 A. C. de Schrevel, *Troubles religieux du XVIe siècle au quartier de Bruges (1566-1568)* (Bruges, 1894), p. 14.

111 De Coussemaker, *op. cit.,* IV, p. 101.

112 Victor Fris, *Geschiedenis van Geeraardsbergen* (Ghent, 1911), p. 177.

113 *Broer Cornelis . . . ,* fol. 201; H. Q. Janssen, *De Kerkhervorming te Brugge* (Rotterdam, 1856), I, p. 34; H. Broecx van Groenen, "Uit het verleden der Doopsgezinden te Aardenburg" in *Doopsgezinde Bijdragen,* IV (1864), p. 84 f.

Jooris de Backere admitted having been baptized in 1567 in Bruges; this testifies to the presence there of a functioning congregation. (Ghent City, *Crime,* 1572-74, fol. 89.)

114 Verheyden, *Bruges,* Nos. 50-60.

115 Van Braght, *Mirror,* II, p. 367.

tioned above, this very close co-operation had serious disadvantages, and the Flemish groups never ceased to desire a bishop from and for their own country, who would, according to the old regulations of Menno Simons, "travel throughout the country during a certain part of the year, to baptize those who were ready [i.e., those who finished their probation years and were willing to receive baptism] or, if they have been baptized before by others, to rebaptize."[116]

The journeys of Leenaert Bouwens of 1554-56, 1557-61, and 1563-65 prove that at that time Flanders had not yet risen beyond the status of an ecclesiastical province, subsumed under the general structure of Northern Netherlands Mennonitism. The less educated local leaders did the difficult and very dangerous work of recruiting and training the converts. They prepared them for the arrival of the Northern elder who after a thorough but necessarily short investigation would decide whether to baptize.

After 1566, however, the continuing and paralyzing religious disputes began in the Mennonite North, occupying the leaders almost continuously. From now on, the North would not forsake Flanders, would never cease to help, especially financially, but only very seldom would send leaders on a systematic trip through the Flemish country, not even in periods of relative religious freedom.

Fortunately thirty-six years of preaching the faith had in the meantime raised up capable workers in Flanders. Now native elders were able to assist the Flemish Mennonites in counsel and in deed. A long-cherished hope had found fulfillment. If ever again a Northerner came to Flanders his influence would no longer equal that of the native leaders, to say nothing of his being able to force upon them his own views. This ability to stand firmly on their own feet saved the South from the tragic divisions of the North. The unity of the Flemish brotherhood, strengthened by manifold sufferings, remained fundamental in the smallest as well as the largest groups.

Thus it is not strange that there were here no large-scale divisions, nor any noticeable success on the part of David Joris or Adam Pastor, although both schismatics visited the country.[117] Unchallenged and, what is more important, united, Pauwels van Meenen and Hans Busschaert now assumed the leadership in Flanders.

Pauwels, born of a prominent family in Meenen, has been described as "a tallish man with a brown beard."[118] Since we may assume that he

116 Vos, DtA, p. 333.
117 B.R.N., II, p. 223.
118 Vos, op. cit., p. 358; Bruges State, Crim. Bouck, 1561-68, fol. 167vo.

was an elder by the end of 1567 or early 1568, he must have been a member of the movement for some time previous to this date. The office of elder was not entrusted to untested novices. He very probably had previously done good work in his personal preaching and contributed to the success of Mennonitism in the southern part of the Flemish province. His wealthy background presupposes also a good education, by reason of which it was probably not too difficult for him to become a capable preacher. It may thus be assumed that he was ordained to the office of baptizer by the Flemish brotherhoods after giving proof of sound and sincere convictions.

People known to have been baptized by him in the beginning of his career are Baudewynken, who joined the brotherhood at Hondschoote,[119] Jan van Akkeren, accepted in the vicinity of Halewijn in the presence of fifty persons,[120] and Calleken Claus, baptized by him at Ghent together with a number of others who are not named.[121] In this city he also performed the marriage of Cattelyne van Hulle and Jacob Martens.[122]

Just as Pauwels van Meenen preferred to be in the South, his colleague, Hans Busschaert, visited the congregations in Northern Flanders. A native of Dadizele, he was described by Herman Vlekwijk in 1565 as "a man with a small beard" close to forty years of age. After 1565 Hans had taken the place of Leenaert Bouwens. His presence was most noticeable at Ghent. Here it was that he baptized Herman Vlekwijk, the faithful friend of Jacques de Rore, together with eight other believers.[123]

Besides these two leaders special mention should be made of Jacques de Rore, surnamed the Candlemaker (de Kaarsgieter), for his tireless defense of Mennonite teachings.[124] That we do not place him on the same level as Pauwels van Meenen and Hans Busschaert is justified by his own statement; he insisted that he never baptized anyone, but only called people to the meetings and sometimes spoke there. Nevertheless he was probably, if not the best-read, at least one of the most zealous propagandists of Mennonitism who ever worked in Flanders. The known facts about his life follow.

Jacques de Rore was born at Courtrai in 1532 of a working man's family. His father was by profession a chandler, whence Jacques received his surname. Like many of his countrymen he chose the weaver's pro-

119 Ghent City, *Crime*, 1572-74, fol. 26.
120 Vos, *op. cit.*, p. 358.
121 Ghent City, *Crime*, 1572-74, fol. 50vof.
122 *Ibid.*, 1591-94, fol. 51 f.
123 Bruges State, *Crim. Bouck*, 1569-73, fol. 10.
124 Verheyden, *Bruges*, No. 63.

fession. Perhaps it was in the workshop that Jacques first heard about the new teachings. One thing is sure, however; before he was nineteen years old, he had Mennonite leanings. In 1551 he left the Catholic Church under the influence of Laurens van Gelder (later executed at Antwerp) and Simoen van Leerberghe, and lived from then on in Mennonite circles. Instructed in the new faith, he appeared four years later with some others before Gillis van Aken in the woods of Marken (near Courtrai) to be baptized. From the very beginning he gave promise of becoming more than a simple member. After first serving as a messenger (the member who called the brethren to a meeting), he soon had a leading function in the brotherhood at Courtrai. Perhaps it was he who prepared the way for Leenaert Bouwens' work in Courtrai. It seems likely that on the occasion of the baptismal ceremony in 1557 several of his converts appeared for baptism by the Northern elder. From Courtrai Jacques visited many places in Flanders, among them Meenen, Wervik, Roeselaere, Ypres, Tielt, Ghent and vicinity, Armentières, and Bruges. After 1566 he hid in the latter town till 1568 and contributed his part to the growth of the Mennonite brotherhood there, much to the grief of Friar Cornelis.

When the spy services of the Duke of Alva went into full action, a longer stay in the West Flemish capital seemed impossible for Jacques. He left the country and traveled without incident to Cleve, but did not stay there long. Early in 1569 he was in Gelderland, where he met Herman Vlekwijk. Herman told Jacques that he would soon return to Flanders for business reasons. The temptation to visit his former field of labor was too strong for Jacques. In April of the same year we find both men in Bruges. This journey was to be fatal for both of them, since they were arrested by the agents of Alva.

Until his martyrdom Jacques stood in the service of the brotherhood. From the dungeon he consoled his wife, encouraging her to give their children a Christian education. Again he exhorted the brethren to be tolerant and warned Pauwels van Meenen to be careful with the use of the ban.

Jacques' appearance before Friar Cornelis must have been particularly moving. This archenemy of the Mennonites knew that the man standing before him had struck hard blows at Catholicism not only in South Flanders but also in Bruges. He tried everything to humiliate the Mennonite but never succeeding in shaking his convictions. Jacques de Rore stood true to the faith which he had had the privilege of proclaiming to others for many years. This famous martyr continued to inspire the faithful long after his death; both his letters and the reports of his trials were preserved and were spread far and wide, both by word of mouth and in printed form.

Michielsen Geeryts confessed at Breda (August 22, 1571) to the possession of a separate edition of the "letters of Jacques the Candlemaker executed at Bruges in the year '69 on July 10." He had bought this booklet shortly before from a young man who had brought it to him in his home at Zierikzee. Joos de Tollenaere—hanged at Ghent on April 13, 1589—wrote to his daughter during his stay in prison that her mother should give her some Mennonite writings to read, and among others "a booklet of Jacques the Candlemaker."[125]

Under the capable leadership of the trio, Pauwels van Meenen, Hans Busschaert, and Jacques de Rore, there must have been a legion of simple, convinced witnesses whose quiet work brought about countless conversions. Only exceptionally are their names known. Besides Clays de Commere, Franchois Feryn, Gillis de Poortere, Michiel Verhage, Zacharias, Adriaen Lhermite, Loys the Teacher,[126] many will remain anonymous for all time. Of Jan Kerbusch it is known that he was teaching and baptizing in South Flanders in 1566.[127] But all of them worked together through these years to bring the brotherhood to a high point and assure a solid foundation for the future. Thus when Flanders was represented at the Mennonite assembly in Hoorn in 1567, this representation had behind it a flourishing brotherhood. To be exact, it is difficult to determine whether Hans Busschaert at that time represented the congregations in Flanders or the refugees from Flanders and Brabant living in the North; but this distinction is unimportant, since the viewpoints of these two groups corresponded in the desire to defend the authority of the congregation against certain authoritative individuals. To follow further this question would, however, lead into a doctrinal discussion concerning matters already dealt with in the introduction. What interests us here is the fact that the Flemish Mennonites were strongly represented in the North around 1568.

Without doubt the beginnings of this "Flemish colony" go back to 1551. The general dispersion which took place at that time has already been described, when dozens of Mennonites had to leave all the major centers in great haste. Many of them settled permanently in the North, especially those who could find employment or whose financial resources permitted a new start. This wave of migration, second in importance only to the one caused by the Spanish Restoration under Alessandro

125 Van Braght, *Mirror*, II, p. 777.

126 Bruges State, *Crim. Bouck*, 1561-68, fol. 2 f., 163vof.

127 On April 30, 1567, Simon de Gruntere declared to his questioners at Sint-Winnoxbergen "that he had never heard the preaching [i.e., attended the meetings] of the Anabaptists, but had heard once or twice an exhortation concerning them, by a certain Jan Kerbusch, a leading baptizer."

Farnese, sprang from the drastic intervention of Alva. The new governor acted upon orders from Philip II, who, angered by the vigorous resistance of the Dutch to his absolutism and repression, saw in the Iconoclasm an opportunity to restore his and the Catholic Church's authority in the most brutal way.[128]

Philip found in Alva the ideal instrument for this undertaking. Fully imbued with his master's intention, the duke did not hesitate to employ most arbitrary methods to attain the ultimate goal, the breaking of all resistance. In addition to dictatorial economic measures (the triple taxation of capital, fixed goods, and personal goods) and similar ones in the political realm (the annihilation of municipal autonomy), the ultimate in absolutism was his institution of the Council for Troubles, popularly called the "Blood Council."[129]

Poullet has rightly said that when Alva went into action the crisis was already past in the Netherlands. Everyone who had had a significant part in the uprising had already fled before the duke's arrival. Nothing in the political situation justified the measures he took; the situation had already returned to normal. Furthermore, the existing tribunals were competent for dealing both with political offenses and with behavior forbidden by the edicts against heresy. The elimination of these institutions meant the trampling underfoot of civil justice and the removal of the king's subjects from the jurisdiction of their own courts to put them at the mercy of the whims of foreign lawyers.

Still the local representation on the Council for Troubles was not insignificant. The chairman was Duke Alva; his deputies were Noircarmes and Berlaymont. The Council consisted further of Adriaan Nicolai, chancellor of Gelderen; Jacob Martens, chairman of the Council of Flanders; Pieter Asset, chairman of the Council of Artois; Juan de Vargas and Luis del Rio, Spaniards; Jan de Blasere, member of the Council of Mechelen; and Jacob Hessels, member of the Council of Flanders. Three magistrates were appointed as prosecuting attorneys: Jan du Bois, Jan de la Porte, and Claude Belin. The secretaries were four secretaries from the Secret Council.

Yet the Dutch members of the Council for Troubles were only figureheads; the real masters were Alva, who pronounced the final verdicts, and the two Spaniards, who alone had the right to vote. The Council functioned according to Philip's desires. Dozens of sentences

---

128 E. Gossaert, "Philippe II a-t-il fait exécuter Egmont et Hornes?" in *Cassandre*, III, No. 22 (May 30, 1936), pp. 3 f.

129 J. Scheerder, *op. cit.*, 96-102; Jamees, *Inventaris van het fonds van Raad van Beroerten* (Brussels, 1958), Introduction.

were pronounced daily; long lists of suspects were transmitted to the magistrates; officers were sent from city to city to supervise the measures against heresy. The non-Catholic population experienced a most dreadful wave of persecution in early 1568. Fully unexpected, a massive raid swept over all Flanders beginning March 3. Alva had laid his plans carefully. On February 21 he had given the necessary instructions to the royal councilors Frans Courtewille and Jan van der Burcht, who were to be responsible for the purge in the province, and on March 3 heretics were seized in every city and town. Sympathizers with the Reformation were dragged into prison by the score. The plan was carried out in complete secrecy; Courtewille and van der Burcht had instructions to deal only with the most trustworthy men within the local governments. A study of the martyrologies for 1568-69 reveals the faithfulness with which the plan was executed.[130]

The mobilization of the Blood Council filled everyone with horror. The greater the distance from Brussels, the more rapidly the zeal of the local authorities diminished, especially after the first rage had subsided. The Northern Netherlands calmed down first; once again this was a place where many settled while waiting for better times. The "Flemish colony" grew visibly in numbers and became an appreciable factor in the Northern brotherhood.

Still this movement was not sufficiently great to cripple the Mennonite churches in the South. That large-scale meetings were abandoned is natural, considering the new measures of control. But in the cities the brethren defied the spies and continued to hold small meetings with the most trustworthy members.[131] In the smaller centers those Mennonites who remained were no longer able to meet. Yet all these faithful, in town or city, nonetheless maintained their bonds with one another. This was of the greatest importance for the fugitives who stayed within the country, seeking safety by a continual change of domicile,[132] because they

130 Brussels Royal, *EA*, reg. 499, fol. 105. Courtewille and van der Burcht were especially charged with carrying out the operation. They were instructed to contact Alonso de Ulloa, captain of the local garrison. The lists of ban and confiscation warrants which they drew up in November, 1568, contain the following names of Mennonites who had fled: Martin Liebaert, Jehan de Smit, Arnoult Steyaert (these three with their wives); Olivier and Jehenne van Lovendegem, Jehenne and Cateline van Hulle, Jehenna Spreekaert, Simon de Roo, Mathieu Standaert, Jehan Buus, George de Kesele. *(Ibid.,* reg. 530, fol. 283 f.)

131 Guillaume van de Daele, summoned to testify concerning some accused Mennonites, was himself trapped when the court required him to take the oath. (Ghent City, *Crime,* 1561-63, p. 154.)

132 Ths strategy is not new. On October 27, 1561, during the previous period of persecution, Titelman wrote, "They keep their activities, their doctrine, and [the identity of] their converts so secret that, not being informed of their activities, one can do hardly anything

knew in advance where they could go. Jacob van de Wege—arrested and burned at the stake in Ghent in 1573—had in this way succeeded in evading the authorities for seven years; he had hidden "with good friends here and there in Flanders."[133]

The dangers faced by the fugitives should, however, not be underestimated. City officials were required by edict to investigate closely all newcomers; a stranger became the object immediately of multiple inquiries. If found not to be in irreproachable standing with the church, he could expect immediate arrest. Fourteen Mennonites were imprisoned in Bruges in February, 1568, "all strangers, having taken up residence in said city [Bruges]."[134] A sentence pronounced on December 9, 1568, confirms this observation; few of the thirty-two banished, and none of the thirteen condemned to death, were from Bruges.[135] What has been observed here for Bruges may be said as well for other cities; the martyr lists make abundantly clear that in the period 1566 to 1569 very few were sentenced at their places of birth.

In spite of all these dangers the brotherhood stood firm. It has already been noted that meetings continued in the cities and were temporarily halted only in the smaller towns. More and more meetings came to be held outside the cities, preferably in wooded areas. Even Bruges, which was most dangerous by reason of the five hundred soldiers per-

against them; even more so because they succeed in seducing many, and if we arrest one household, the others go elsewhere and within one or two weeks have numerous sympathizers and proselytes" (Gaillard, op. cit., p. 224).

133 As hiding places he mentioned Meenen, Halewijn, and Wervik, and gave the impression that these were but a few examples. (Van Braght, Mirror, II, p. 648.)

134 Bruges City, Varia, anno 1567 (1568 n.st.). [Translator's note: The "new style" dating is that in which the new year is counted as beginning on January 1. The sixteenth century used three ways of dating the beginning of a year. One could begin with Christmas (modo nativitatis), so that the last week of December, 1567, was counted as part of 1568; or with the conception of Christ (modo incarnationis or stilo gallie), so that the period from January 1 to March 25, 1568, was still counted as part of 1567. The "new style," counting January 1 as the hinge between the years (modo circumcisionis), was just in the process of being accepted because of its greater simplicity, in spite of its lesser theological merit.] This document is a petition of July 27, 1568, in favor of nine Mennonites who had recanted. The other five remained steadfast. Some of those for whom grace is requested are named: Mailart de Grave with his wife Valentyne Ryckele and their three children, Lievin van den Berghe, Pieter Gheive, and Maria Lowers. The three children, Lievin van den Berghe, and Maria Lowers escaped the death penalty. (Cf. Verheyden, Bruges, pp. 55 f.)

A loose sheet from the same collection (Varia, anno 1576) emphasizes still more the immigration of out-of-town Mennonites: "it having been found that all those infected with heresy, as long as one can remember, have been strangers, neither from the city nor from its immediate surroundings."

135 Bruges City, Hallegeboden, 1564-74, fol. 180vof.; A. C. de Schrevel, Troubles religieux du XVIe siècle au quartier de Bruges, used this document without citing the source. A list of persons summoned by Alva, which de Schrevel also printed with no indication of source (pp. 280 f.), is found on fol. 130voff.

manently stationed there since 1565 with the assignment of raiding every known meeting,[136] was no exception to this rule. Undismayed by this small army, the faithful Mennonites met in the Tillegem wood—barely two miles from the city—under the leadership of Willem Verron.[137] On the afternoon of Ascension Day, May 4, 1570, they were surprised there near the castle of Lady Anna of Ostend. Many, among them the preacher, were nonetheless able to escape. Those trapped were Willem Verron, born in Diksmuide, citizen of Brussels, sculptor by trade; his son Pieter; Karel de Raedt, born in Courtrai; Hans Schaeck, likewise from Courtrai; Hendrik Joorissen de Graedt, born in Middelburg (Zeeland); Jacquemynkin, the daughter of Gerard de Backere, citizen of Bruges, goldsmith.

In spite of the repeated court sessions, the investigators were unable to obtain any useful information. The following text from the record of the hearings is clear: "Refuse to name any of their accomplices or teachers, notwithstanding whippings already administered and threats of further torture." All that the judges learned was that meetings had been held regularly since 1565.

To generalize for all Flanders this unbroken continuity would be unrealistic. Through the dispersion many a smaller group was threatened with extinction. It would, however, also be incorrect to generalize in the opposite direction, as did Vos in 1920, that "when Alva's iron hand pressed on the South the congregations gave way one after the other."[138] Nothing could be less true. The reader of the *Martyrs' Mirror* can ascertain that during the period 1569 to 1574 the inquisitors never ceased to have work at Ghent, Courtrai, Ypres, Meenen, Tielt, and Asper.[139] Jacques de Rore may well have spoken the truth when in answer to questioning about his fellow believers he said that they were "all scattered." Yet when Hans van de Wege was led to the Vrijdagmarkt for execution in 1570 there were still brethren there to greet him and call to him, "Hold fast!" and "Fight aright for the truth!"[140]

This public manifestation of sympathy drove the Ghent authorities

---

136 Bruges City, *Varia*, anno 1565.

137 Bruges State, *Brugsche Vrije-Parochies en Heerlijkheden*, Tillegem, No. 30: "Memori nopende zeker herdoopers ende andere ghevanghen ter deser heerlichede." This document was lent by the archivist, Dr. L. van Werveke, to whom I here express my gratitude.

138 It should no longer be necessary to refute the view of H. Pirenne, *Histoire de Belgique*, IV (Brussels, 1919), p. 124, who claims that after 1566 Protestantism was extinct in Belgium. According to Pirenne, who follows the biased thesis of Kervyn de Lettenhove, the Calvinistic regime of 1578-85 was nothing but a *coup d'état* of returning emigrants.

139 Josse Tam was burned at Hondschoote on October 20, 1571 (de Coussemaker, *Troubles*, IV, p. 211 f.)

140 Van Braght, *Mirror*, II, p. 528.

to action. The next day they announced a prize of fifty carolus-guilders to anyone who would denounce one of the demonstrators.[141] It had become evident to the city government that the Mennonites had not given up the struggle, but that unknown to the authorities an undeniable regrouping of the remaining forces had taken place. Other testimonies to the same effect can be cited.

The chronicler de Jonghe, commenting on the arrest of Mennonites in 1573, says that the government had been able to lay hands on a book "in which were the names and surnames of those who gave weekly gifts for the expenses of the poor within their sect."[142] Mattheus Bernaert, who was "a minister of the church of God, in the Word of the holy Gospel, and also in the deacon's office," may well have been one of the prisoners in this group.[143] In 1574 it was discovered (did one of the prisoners talk too much?) that the local congregation had regular contact with the believers in Zeeland. A search was ordered for Gillis de Bruyckere, the bearer of letters from the congregation at Rassen.[144]

In late 1572 or early 1573 Pauwels van Meenen visited Ghent to administer baptism. The twenty-two-year-old Adriaen van der Zwalme (arrested at Bruges and executed there August 7, 1573), one of those baptized by Pauwels, confessed that the ceremony had been attended by twenty or thirty people. The bare fact that the brotherhood dared to hold a meeting of that size in the city proper is ample proof that the crisis had once more been surmounted.[145] Nor was this true only at Ghent. Maurissus van Dale of Bellem declared that in 1572 "a minister and teacher from Friesland made a trip through Flanders."[146] Such a journey would have been senseless had not the baptizer, whom we cannot identify, known in advance that the work to be done would justify the risks. Maurissus van Dale must have been quite active himself as well,

---

141 Ghent City, *Crime*, 1572-74, fol. 103vo; *Resolutiën*, 1571-74, fol. 103vo; *Serie 93 bis*, reg. E.E., fol. 30vo.

142 De Jonghe, *Ghent*, I, p. 215.

143 Van Braght, *Mirror*, II, p. 623. Might this Mattheus have been related to Gillis and Michiel Beernaerts, Mennonite teachers in the Antwerp area? (Vos, *DtA*, pp. 333, 358.)

144 Ghent City, *KR*, 1571-74, fol. 192, June 20, 1573.

145 Bruges State, *Crim. Bouck*, 1573-83, fol. 10. Adriaen van der Zwalmen had previously been arrested at Ghent and had recanted. Soon, however, he repented of his cowardice and returned to the brotherhood. For a time he took refuge in Dordrecht, and was captured soon after his return to Flanders. He was burned together with Mattheus Knese at Bruges. (Verheyden, *Bruges*, p. 63.)

146 Ghent City, *Series 206 (Examinaciën en Sententiën door den Souverein balliu in 't quartier van gend, 1573-1574)*, fol. 53vo. On January 5, 1572, Pierijntgen Neckers was burned at the stake at Meenen, ample proof that also in Southern Flanders Mennonites had not given up the fight. (Van Braght, *Mirror*, II, p. 641.)

to be called "the bishop of the Anabaptists" by his neighbors.[147] Another noteworthy apostle in this period was Christoffel van Leuven; as "minister of the Word of God" he visited the Flemish brotherhood and was especially active around Ghent.[148]

When the Reformation in general had encountered better times and a Calvinistic regime was about to be set up, Mennonitism had again sunk roots deep into the Flemish soil.[149] It was ready to face new problems and to conquer the bitterest of disappointments, namely, the refusal of other Reformation confessions (when they came into power) to recognize the Mennonite brotherhood.

147 Ghent City, *Series 206*, fol. 532vo.

148 Van Braght, *Mirror*, II, p. 648.

149 In 1574 Joos Steyaert declared that he had attended Mennonite meetings not only at Ghent but also elsewhere. (Ghent City, *Examinaciën, 1573-74*, fol. 148.) This reconsolidation of the churches went on in the face of unrelenting persecution. The civil authorities had been ordered to stand permanently by the ecclesiastical bloodhounds. If a hardened heretic was turned over to the magistrate, the latter was required to pronounce sentence immediately and turn him over to the hangman within twenty-four hours. Further, the heretics should henceforth be prevented from speaking on their way to the place of execution by burning their tongues with red-hot irons. Stadsarchiv Ghent, *Keure-Resolutiën, 1571-74*, fol. 54 f.)

III. THE PERIOD OF
RELATIVE FREEDOM: 1576-1586

During this period the hostilities between Catholics and Calvinists flared up in full force. When occasionally a common political interest brought them together, the religious differences, which lay as a chasm between them, always destroyed the truce and brought the two parties again into conflict. In the study of the events of this period it becomes evident that religion and politics form an integral whole. What we shall observe is more than the struggle of the Reformation against the reaction of church and state; it is at the same time the common struggle of the people of the Netherlands for political emancipation, a struggle completely successful in the North, but only moderately so in the South.

The sudden death of the governor Requescens, whose administration had permitted a revival of Calvinism, created political confusion, which was to lead to the first reconcilation of the Calvinistic North with the Catholic South. Since Requescens had not been able to appoint a successor, the Council of State itself was the proper organ to govern in the name of Philip II until the king could appoint a new governor. This should have guaranteed the necessary continuity. But it soon became evident that the Council was inadequate. Its members—Viglius, the Duke of Aarschot, the Count of Berlaymont, the Baron of Ressenghien, Assonleville, Sasbout, and Mansfeld—were too old or incapable of bearing such a responsibility. Philip knew that, although they themselves were loyal to the church and the crown, they would attempt, even at the cost of compromise, to reach an understanding between the Catholic and Protestant blocs. For this reason the king bypassed the Council and corresponded secretly with Geronimo de Roda, assessor in the "Blood Council," who had been Requescens' confidant until his death. De Roda, also a member of the Council of State, was a stubborn advocate of Spanish absolutism and of the Catholic Church; hence there was no danger that he would make concessions to the other camp. Willing instrument in the hands of the Madrid government, he was feared and shunned both by his fellow councilors and by the people.

The inactivity of the Council of State gave William of Orange an occasion to seek to unite the North and the South and to free the Netherlands from Spain. The arrest of the members of the Council of State and the coup d'état of the Brabant estates were the milestones in the development which led to the signature of the Pacification of Ghent on November 8, 1576.[1] As important as was the political basis of the Pacification as a symptom of the desire of the people to throw off the Spanish yoke, the question of religious freedom was to be of more conclusive significance in the struggle for a durable unity.

Seen in this light, the Pacification did not produce the desired results. Their signatures notwithstanding, both parties had retained their respective religious conceptions. The Catholics hoped to undo in the future the rights conceded to Calvinism in the North, and their adversaries never ceased to be offended by the fact that Reformed doctrines could not be preached in the South. The Ghent agreement cannot be considered as an ecclesiastical peace treaty; it was no more than a truce, accepted while waiting for conditions which would enable a final settlement.

The Union of Brussels, signed on January 9, 1577, brought an initial clarification in a strictly anti-Calvinistic direction. Superficially the Union is simply a confirmation of the Pacification. It speaks explicitly of the unanimous determination of the signers to resist "the Spanish tyranny . . . on pain of losing title, name, arms, and honor; of being regarded by God and everyman as perjurers, faithless, enemies of our fatherland, eternally marked as infamous and cowardly." But, in reality, this document was intended to crush definitively the Calvinist cause in the South. The text itself gives as one of the reasons for the necessity of the Union, "the conservation of our Holy and Apostolic Roman Catholic Religion and Faith."[2]

The Union is, as Pirenne has remarked, both a national and a Catholic union.[3] Fortunately for the Calvinists, Don Juan was unable, upon his arrival in the Netherlands, to take advantage of this Catholic strength. In his haste to end the revolt, the new governor so displeased his fellow Catholics that co-operation between Catholics and Calvinists again became possible. This merger of all the Netherlands compelled Don Juan, in spite of his initial military successes, to retreat to Namur.

---

1 Henri Pirenne, *Histoire de Belgique,* IV, pp. 60-82. The text of the Pacification appears in A. Anselmo, ed., *Placcaeten van Brabant,* I (Antwerp, 1648), pp. 586-95, and in French translation in Theodore Juste, *La Pacification de Gand,* pp. I-XLVIII.

2 J. C. de Jonghe, *De Unie van Brussel des jaars 1577, naar het oorspronkelijke uitgegeven* (The Hague, 1825). Besides a brief introduction concerning the character and significance of the treaty, the author has compiled biographical data on each of the 257 signers. (Pp. 34-206.)

3 Pirenne, *op. cit.,* IV, p. 90.

He thus made room for William of Orange, whom the South greeted as a liberator.

The political situation being thus clarified, the religious problem came into focus again. Division threatened more seriously than ever, since both parties sensed that a conclusive settlement was nearing and sought to defend their respective interests to the uttermost. The Prince of Orange sought to dampen this fierce particularism and urged both camps toward tolerance. His "Religionsfrid,"[4] roughly a second Pacification of Ghent, submitted to the States on July 10, 1578, gave Calvinists the right to exercise their religion freely, but in turn forbade them to attack the Catholics. But the dictatorial tendencies of the Calvinist leaders of Ghent and Antwerp made any durable agreement impossible. The Catholics soon became the victims of divers kinds of discrimination, which progressively grew into real persecution. At that point the alliance fell apart. The division could then be used by the new governor, Alessandro Farnese, to promote his plans for a reconquest.

In the midst of these constant realignments of forces, now to the advantage of the Catholics, now in favor of the Calvinists, Mennonitism found itself in an extraordinary position between 1576 and 1586. The masses followed with intense interest the struggle between the two parties, with popular sympathies increasingly on the side of the Calvinists.[5] When the religious struggle became intertwined with the revolt against Spanish absolutism the common man was still more militantly ready to defend his rights. Political and religious life was uniformly dominated by a nerve-racking atmosphere of partisanship. This was hardly a favorable situation for the Mennonites, who sought to unite humanity in a spirit of brotherly love. Such a message must have had an anachronistic ring and seemed all too lukewarm for those with dreams of domination. For the great majority, whether Catholic or Calvinist, the primary concern was to gain control in city and country; purely religious issues took second place. That the brethren carried on their activities in the shadow of these conflicts without becoming involved in the political complications of the religious struggle was to have serious consequences for them. When the various religious truces were drawn up, the interests of Calvin-

---

4 Canon Florent Prims, *De Religionsvrede, 1578-1581* (Antwerp, 1942).

5 At Ypres the magistrate was compelled to intervene against the wearing of "foxtails . . . to the scandal and displeasure of all decent people" (A. C. de Schrevel, *Recueil de Documents relatifs aux troubles religieux en Flandre, 1577-85*) (Bruges, 1921-28, I, pp. 307 f.). In Bruges the story was the same. A prohibition had to be decreed against "calling names such as 'papist' or 'Protestant' or other such quarreling or scoffing words and epithets or any kind of gossip by either side, against and in infraction of the Pacification of Ghent" (Bruges City, *Hallegeboden*, April 5, 1578).

ists and Catholics were taken into account, but the Mennonites were never mentioned. Not one of the agreements—the Pacification, the Union, or the Religionsfrid—recognized them. The appeals for mutual toleration applied only to Calvinists and Catholics. The Mennonites continued to be regarded as not belonging to Christian society, so that, even if events had taken a different turn, the brotherhood would still not have been granted the right to exist.

Yet even though not one of the twenty-five articles of the Pacification was meant for them, it cannot be denied that the treaty brought the Mennonites great advantages. Freedom of movement throughout the Netherlands (Article IV) allowed numerous emigrants to return to their former fields of activity. No longer would the fearsome "blood edicts" embitter their life in the South (Article V). With rejoicing the brethren who had escaped the clutches of the police must have greeted their imprisoned brethren at the opened prison gates (Article IX). Many may have been able to reclaim confiscated goods (Articles X, XIV, XV, XVI, XVIII, XIX, XXII).

Except for the return of the emigrants (probably a result of the changed political situation rather than of the provisions of Article V of the Pacification), these concessions were not applied immediately. The Union of Brussels, signed a few months later, actually brought new restrictions to Protestants in the South; the brief Catholic resistance was for a time insuperable. The Pacification was not effectively applied until its confirmation by the Religionsfrid. Only then could the above-mentioned privileges really be enjoyed.

In spite of the fact that the Religionsfrid referred only to two confessions, the Calvinist and the Catholic, the Mennonites no doubt profited by the regulations in Article VII. This article read: "And if said services are not held in public, no one shall be questioned or interfered with in any way in religious matters concerning what he does within his home."[6] None of the other twenty-nine articles of the Religionsfrid is as important as this one, not even Articles III and IV, which provided that the believers of one of the recognized confessions could own church buildings only if they were represented at a given place by at least one hundred families domiciled there at least a year. The brethren were left out of account because of the fanatical attitude of their opponents. Besides, however great an expansion Mennonitism may have known in this period or in the preceding one, the quota of one hundred families was certainly seldom attained except in the largest cities. It is worthy of note that the Men-

6 De Jonghe, *op. cit.*, II, p. 279.

nonites at Ghent actually petitioned the magistrate to designate certain churches for their use. If this step indicates that they had reached the quota of one hundred families, Articles III and IV of the Religionsfrid were not useless to them; such a deduction would also permit us to fix approximately the number of Mennonites in the city.

Though comparable information is not available for Bruges, it is very probable that the Mennonites there would also have been able to make such a request. Bruges was by no means the Catholic city it had been in times past. The magistrate had little to answer to the accusations made in 1576 by the Dominican monk Alfonso of St. Emilian[7] and the Augustinian Lorenço Villavicencio.[8] Alfonso wrote to Philip II: "Said city is completely infected by said heretical pest more than any other city of the region, even more than the city of Geneva; it is a refuge and a storehouse of all heretics and miscreants. Of a thousand homes in that city not one is pure." Lorenço Villavicencio had even before this, in a bitingly critical writing, attacked the weak government of the city, which he pictured as completely heretical. Although Alfonso and Villavicencio explicitly mentioned the Calvinists only, both of them must have known that the growth of Protestantism was always accompanied by a revival of Mennonitism. Did not Alfonso testify that Bruges was a gathering place for *all* heretics? Their descriptions confirm what Friar Cornelis had said not too long before, on February 15, 1568, concerning the number of Mennonites in the city: "Their devilish congregation is at least 700 strong here in the city of Bruges."

Notwithstanding the workings of the inquisitorial power—from 1568 to 1573 twenty Mennonites were handed over to the executioner in Bruges[9]—as soon as the Catholics lost their power to the Calvinists, the Mennonites as well were present on the religious scene. This was never more than a "presence." They were never in any way officially recognized, even if it be assumed that the Mennonites of Bruges made an appeal for the right of assembly on the basis of Articles III and IV. That they took such steps, as was done elsewhere in Flanders, is very probable. But like their fellow believers at Ghent, the Mennonites probably met with no success. Everywhere outside their fellowship the brethren encountered suspicion and hostility. We have already mentioned the refusal of Prince William of Orange; to him the mere existence of Mennonite groups was a constant menace to the maintenance of general peace and social order.[10]

---

7 De Schrevel, *op. cit.*, I, pp. 308 f.
8 Bruges City, *Varia*, No. 1576.
9 Cf. Verheyden, *Bruges*.
10 In 1579, when the negotiations leading toward the Religionsfrid were in a critical

As for the Catholic population, besides their aversion to any non-Catholic confession, they hated most violently those whom they still called the "Münsterites."

The Calvinists who were in power for the moment were bent on ecclesiastical monopoly and were hardly inclined to heed any such requests from the Mennonites. In their synodal session at Antwerp on February 2, 1576, the following resolution was adopted: "The assembled brethren hold and believe that the Anabaptists do not believe rightly in Jesus Christ, according to the Word of God, and if they persist to the end in their error, without being converted by God, that they will not be saved, according to the testimonies of the Scriptures."[11] Consequently, nothing but opposition could be expected from the Calvinistic leaders, even during the period of the Religionsfrid.

Jacobus Regius, the minister of the Reformed Church at Ghent from 1577 until October, 1584, is typical of the untiring adversaries of Mennonitism. He wrote in 1575: "Oh, that God would some time crush this sect!"[12] To him there was, besides Catholicism, no teaching more pestiferous than that of Menno Simons and his followers. He left no means untried to prevent the spreading of this faith,[13] while awaiting the time when it would be completely destroyed. Great was his enthusiasm when his colleague and friend in Delft, Arent Cornelis, sent him some pamphlets which in simple language attacked the Mennonite teachings. Jacobus Regius was convinced that it would be of little use to have debates between theologians with the intent of winning those infected by Mennonitism, and that a clear and simple pamphlet would be more effective than the most sensational debate.

Perhaps less ardent, but no less convinced, was Petrus Dathenus, though he found it necessary to vigorously deny a report that he was inclined to make certain concessions to David Joris' type of Anabaptism.[14] The Frankenthal (Germany) debate of 1571, which lasted for months, where he disputed with fifteen Mennonites, gives ample proof of his feel-

phase, the Prince of Orange is reported to have expressed the following opinion on the Mennonites: "seditious, disobedient, disloyal, incompatible people with whom it is impossible to live in unity and peace" (Lettres d'un gentilhomme, vray patriot, à Messieurs les Estatz Généraulx assemblez en la ville d'Anvers), fol. b 2vo.

11 N. C. Kist and H. J. Royaarts, Archief voor kerkelijke geschiedenis (Leiden, 1829-49), XX, p. 168.

12 F. Pijper, Nederlandsch archief voor kerkgeschiedenis, nieuwe serie, VII (1909), p. 19.

13 On October 20, 1573, he informed Arent Cornelis that its doctrines had been spread throughout Belgium. (Ibid., 20.)

14 H. Q. Janssens, "Petrus Dathenus op den avond van zijn leven. Een bezoek bij hem te Staden," in Bijdragen tot de oudheidkunde en geschiedenis, inzonderheid van Zeeuwsch-Vlaanderen (Middelburg, 1856-63), III, pp. 1-16.

ings. In him the Calvinists had an excellent advocate who lost no opportunity for combat.

The most formidable of the enemies of the brethren was, however, Marnix of St. Aldegonde. This faithful friend of William of Orange shared the prince's views on the matter of Mennonitism. Several times in 1566 William had proposed to the regent, Margaret of Parma, that she prohibit such teachings; Marnix was now no longer friendly. Preoccupied with political affairs, this strict Calvinist and practical statesman did not until 1595 work on his notorious *Ondersoeckinge ende grondelijcke wederlegginge der geestdrijvische leere* (Investigation and Thorough Refutation of the Fanatical Doctrine).[15] In speaking of "fanatical doctrine," Marnix, of course, made no distinction between revolutionary Anabaptism and peaceful Mennonitism. All that he writes here could have been written by a Catholic author. He emphasized the revolutionary phase of Anabaptism and with equal zeal discussed the divisions in the Mennonite brotherhood in the Northern Netherlands. His treatment of David Joris' *Wonderboeck,* of Hendrik Claessen's *Evangelium des Rijcks* and *Spiegel der gerechticheyt,* of the *Paradys des vredes* by "another bird of the feather," of Hendrik Jonszen's *Verborgen Ackerschat,* of Sebastian Franck's *Paradoxan* and *Boom der Wetenschap,* as well as of numerous other publications like Niclaes' *Het Huys der Liefden,* had the same purpose. In his earlier anti-Catholic polemic work, *Byenkorf der H. Roomsche Kercke* (1569), he used his customary satirical language. "It is an old proverb," Marnix wrote, "that where the Lord our God establishes a church, the devil builds a chapel beside it." For Marnix the "Devil's Chapel" was naturally Anabaptism.

As William the Silent had once made an appeal to Margaret of Parma, so Marnix now knocked at the door of the States-General in 1595. He urged them to apply without hesitation the most severe restrictive measures to the "Münsterites," "that such a vile and murderous poison may not progress . . . but may be completely suppressed and annihilated." This was the first time Marnix had expressed himself so explicitly against the Mennonites, even advocating "corporal punishment" —a kind of Protestant inquisition—for them. Yet this attitude was consistent with the extremely one-sided Calvinism which could be observed in Marnix two decades earlier, at the beginning of the period under discussion.[16]

15 P. Frédéricq, *Marnix en zijne Nederlandsche geschriften* (Ghent, 1881), pp. 98-109.

16 Marnix' attitude in the time of the negotiations leading to the Religionsfrid may be ascertained from two pamphlets which he wrote at that time: *Supplicatie aen syn Hoocheyt ende Heeren des Raets van State, overgegeven door de inwoonders deser Nederlanden, welcke*

Caught between the two antagonistic religio-political parties, without much relation to either of them, the Mennonites resumed their preaching work on a larger scale. Though they were pursued by the hostility of their opponents on both sides,[17] they were nonetheless free from serious threats of the torture room, the stake, the gallows, or drowning. That the Mennonites felt relatively free during this time is evident in the letter written by Joos de Tollenaere (hanged at Ghent on April 13, 1589) to the brethren of the North, admonishing them not to underestimate the benefit of the freedom they enjoyed. He warned them that sudden disaster might destroy their accustomed security, and that the storm might break at the most unexpected moment, "as now in Flanders, where we also had such freedom, for about seven years."[18] Joos thereby was referring to the period from 1577-78 to 1585. This date 1577-78

protesteren dat sy begeren te leven nae de reformatie des Evangeliums (addressed to Don Mathias on June 22, 1578) and Vermaninghe ende Raet voor de Nederlanden, waer in doorsake bewesen wort van den tegenwoordigen inlandschen twist, ende oock de Remedie daer teghen, maer principalyck wort hier bewesen oft men, den Conscientien behoort te bedwinghen. (Both pamphlets appeared in French as well. Concerning Marnix' authorship and his leading role in Antwerp's campaign for a religious truce, cf. Canon Fl. Prims, De Religionsvrede, pp. 59-65.) These pamphlets represent the first public opposition to the Union of Brussels, advocating a solution of the religious problem which conflicted radically with the terms of the 1577 treaty. Marnix identifies the Calvinistic movement with the whole Reformation. Fifty years ago, he declared, some inhabitants of the Netherlands had turned away from Rome. Their number increased visibly, until the time when Alva attempted to reverse the tide by executing 18,000 or 19,000 of them. (Concerning the number of martyrs claimed here and other martyr statistics, cf. the articles in the 1945 volume of Kruisbanier.) That policy failed, however, and Protestantism claimed its rights with increasing force. The Protestants, Marnix said, had at least as much right to freedom as the Jews—the murderers of Jesus Christ—who were even tolerated in the immediate neighborhood of the pope, at least if they purchased the privilege, especially since the Protestants were patriots who always sought the nation's welfare. In short, Marnix' writing is a plea based on well-known themes, ending: "Therefore do the Protestants pray you [Don Mathias] to think about means which will make it possible and admissible for both religions [i.e., Catholic and Calvinist] to be practiced on an equal basis." Marnix does not name the Mennonites, but it is implicit that he has no room for them in his scheme of things. The word "Protestants," which appears fifteen times under his pen, always refers to the Calvinists. Closely related to these pamphlets are two others based on an earlier writing of Marnix' friend du Plessis-Mornay (for bibliographical details, cf. Prims, loc. cit.), whose attitude toward the Mennonites is explicit: " . . . that some of those who are called Anabaptists are opposed in opinion and doctrine to all magistracy, admit no magistracy or government in Christendom, and consequently want to introduce community of goods, is in no way to be allowed, but should be severely punished" (Een vriendelycke vermaninghe tot alle Liefhebbers der Vrijheyt en des religions-vredes, Meulman Collection, No. 365, last two pages).

17 In 1580 an anti-Calvinistic dialogue was published: Een poeetschen Dialogue genaempt Calvinus (Meulman Collection, No. 487). Here the author, who has laid the scene in Hades, puts the following words into Charon's mouth: "The Mennonites were quiet during the crossing; they must be fanatical hypocrites" (P. Frédéricq, Nederlands proza der XVIe eeuw, p. 89).

18 Van Braght, Mirror, II, p. 766.

marks the beginning of the steady decline of Catholic power which led to the Religionsfrid.[19] And 1585, the end of "about seven years," was the date of Alessandro Farnese's assumption of power. In the agreement, which we shall deal with later in more detail, between Farnese as governor and the magistrates of the subjugated cities, all Protestant activities were strictly prohibited. Dissenters again began to be arrested and exiled.

This period of freedom confronts the student of church history with a particularly difficult task. Suddenly all the sources which he could use for the period before 1576 are absolutely silent concerning the Mennonites. The correspondence of the central, provincial, and local governmental authorities, the investigation records concerning particular cases, the trial records (officially in the reports of the councils and bailiffs, anecdotal in van Braght), even the useful though laconic notes in the city financial records, cease to give him information.

This is neither accidental nor illogical. The political leaders, both the Orange party striving for unity and the more particularistically minded Calvinists, were completely occupied with the Catholics. William of Orange was making every possible attempt to avoid a split with the Catholic bloc in the South, while radical Calvinists like the soldier and sea fighter Willem van Hembyze, the preacher Herman Moded, and their followers made life impossible for the very same Catholics. All parties were engaged in a race to secure favorable positions in a very fluid political and religious situation. It is easy to understand that in such a race the Mennonite problem was of minor importance. In the Calvinistic camp it was known that nothing could be expected from the Mennonites by way of support from attack against Catholics, at least as the Calvinists understood such an attack.

On February 21, 1573, in a period during which Protestants were in the minority and therefore a period favorable to the association of non-Catholics, some Calvinistic leaders arranged a secret meeting with the spokesmen of the Mennonites. They conferred on the problem of cooperation in unseating the Catholic domination. Weapons would be necessary "to kill and to pillage the Catholics." The anonymous author of a report about this meeting adds that the conspiracy was not carried out because at that moment ducal armies were concentrated in the region

---

19 Particularly typical of the milder methods in the restriction of heresy was the case of Jan Clincke at Ghent. This Mennonite stubbornly refused to remove his cap at the passing of a procession. Arrested and tortured, he was released with no more than banishment. (Ghent State, *RVBW*, reg. 45, fol. 107, 138-140, 147.)

of Meenen.[20] His statement that the presence of Alva's troops at Meenen probably forced the Calvinists to postpone their plans is acceptable but not his attempt to drag the Mennonites into the plot. Though the lack of clear documentation obliges us to work by hypothesis here, it should be remembered that the Mennonite brotherhood had long since rejected the use of violence. Their resistance to the temptation in 1566 and their attitude during the last years of the century, about which more will be said in the next chapter, testify to their abhorrence of violence. That the Mennonites of 1573 could not accept the proposal of the Calvinists is one more expression of a position which was not motivated by strategic consideration but was integral to their faith.

Because they did not come into question as possible allies in the political aspect of the religious conflict, the Mennonites escaped the attention of a large part of the population of Flanders. Nonetheless, the little we know of the period 1575-85 gives evidence of zealous activity on the part of their evangelists. As has been said, they had gained from the Pacification of Ghent and the Religionsfrid. It was also to their benefit that their activities were considered to be of little importance; they were able to increase their number to a remarkable extent. In 1575 Jacobus Regius had warned of the danger presented by Mennonitism, but his voice was lost in the storm of political events between the various religious "peaces." While the Calvinists succeeded in establishing their rule between 1575 and 1580, the Mennonite brotherhood experienced years of unprecedented prosperity.[21]

At a meeting held in Amsterdam in March, 1581, the Flemish Mennonites were represented by Antwerp and Ghent.[22] The presence of this representation is in itself a significant index of the position which the

20 Ghent City, *Crime*, 1572-74, fol. 59: "On February 21, 1572, was exhibited to the councilmen a note in the French language without address or signature, containing a certain warning that some Calvinists, about eleven of them, who had had contact with the Anabaptists to set a day and arrange for their assistance in weapons to kill and rob the Catholics. . . . This was not done because they would have had to face the duke's troops camped near Meenen. . . ."

21 Details about the growth of Mennonitism in this period are not available. We note, however, the existence of a congregation at Evergem, which was under the leadership of one Zoetart: he had been a monk but in 1576 left the monastery and joined the Mennonites. (De Coussemaker, *Troubles*, I, p. 344.) At Ghent the activities of the Mennonites were not closely watched. In 1576 Raphaël van de Velde urged his brethren in Ghent to leave the city as soon as possible, "for they [the government] are waiting for the right moment, perhaps within a year; they have much on paper" (van Braght, *Mirror*, II, pp. 718 f.).

22 J. Wagenaar, *Amsterdam in zijne opkomst, aanwas* . . . (Amsterdam, 1760-68), VIII, p. 36. Steven Blaupot ten Cate, *Geschiedenis der Doopsgezinden in Holland, Zeeland, Utrecht en Gelderland* (Amsterdam, 1847), I, pp. 34 f. According to this author the gathering was regarded with suspicion by the Reformed clergy.

Flemish churches held in the framework of the Dutch brotherhood. During this four-day meeting a problem of special interest for the Flemish group—perhaps, in fact, the reason for their coming—was dealt with; namely, the ministry to congregations which still had to get along without a permanent pastor.

The Flemish churches were confronted with a thorny problem. On August 1, 1555, it had been decided at Wismar that "no one shall take it upon himself to preach or teach of his own will, if he is not sent or ordained by the congregation or the elder."[23] This resolution still remained in force. Its rigid application had unfavorable results in the South, where the maintenance of contacts between the congregations was always difficult if not in fact dangerous. Many congregations, probably the majority, had to do without a teacher, and there was little chance for improving the situation. Inevitably this led to confusion, and weakened the efforts toward expansion.

The discussions at Amsterdam brought a satisfactory solution. It seems, however, that as far as the South is concerned this solution was simply the acceptance of an already existing situation. As a general rule those congregations that had no teacher available were in the future to have the right to entrust a deacon with the leadership, on condition, however, that his competence and irreproachable character be unchallenged. If it should happen that a congregation could not find a proper teacher among the deacons, the members would have to limit themselves during their meeting to the reading of the Gospel.

In Flanders both these emergency solutions were current. This becomes evident in the fact that after 1585, all the ministers seized by the authorities were "deacon-teachers."

Though less well organized than the Northern congregations, the Flemish brotherhood evangelized so intensively after 1580 that the Calvinists, terrified by the expansion of the "Münsterites," decided in favor of more effective suppression, for members of their own congregations left their ranks to join the Mennonites. One case which must have caused them much grief was that of Michiel de Cleercq, later hanged at Ghent.[24] Though we must discount H. Q. Janssen's statement that Michiel was known already in 1566 as one of the most zealous Calvinists at Eecloo —he was then only fourteen years old—certainly a mere ten years later he may be counted among the best workers of the church at Sluis. In spite of his humble parentage—he was a weaver—the holy fire of preach-

---

23 "Wismar Articles," in Menno Simons, *Complete Writings*, p. 1042, Art. IX.
24 Cf. Verheyden, *Ghent*, pp. 70 f.

ing burned in him. Repeatedly he requested permission to take pastoral responsibilities; every time he was told that he was unqualified for the ministry, probably because of his lack of education. Discouraged, he withdrew in 1580 from the church at Sluis. Janssen, who followed the case of Michiel de Cleercq no further, concluded: "We hear no more of him later; he probably remained inactive." Nothing is less true. Did he go to his home in St. Antelinks (near Aalst) after leaving Sluis? Perhaps. In 1581, at any rate, he was living in Ghent, attracted by Mennonitism.[25] Michiel was baptized in 1588 by Pauwels van Meenen and from then on devoted his best energies to the local Mennonite congregation, filling shortly afterward the office of deacon-teacher.

The case of Michiel de Cleercq certainly was not an isolated one, since the problem of the alarming growth of "the Anabaptists and similar heretics" was placed on the agenda of a provincial synod of the Flemish Reformed churches held on March 8, 1581.[26] The decision made was not very original: if the "Münsterite danger" were to become worse, a debate should be held similar to the one at Frankenthal where Petrus Dathenus had spoken ten years before.

This decision was an indirect acknowledgment that Mennonitism in Flanders could no longer be regarded as a negligible quantity. Though nothing is known of the discussions that went on at the synod concerning this resolution, it may be assumed that serious misgivings were expressed as to the ultimate outcome of continued Mennonite expansion. Many may have feared that the Mennonites, strong even before 1581, would soon demand recognition beside the other confessions and threaten the Calvinistic hegemony.

Early in the following year it became clear that this danger was real. It has already been noted that in 1582 the Mennonites of Ghent emerged from their withdrawal and hiding, and addressed themselves to the authorities, laying claim to the provisions of Article XXV of the Religionsfrid, which obligated the government to deal with all grievances of a religious nature,[27] and requesting authorization to possess a church build-

---

25 "Knows the sect of the Calvinists, having followed and admired them, but after being instructed, he thought that this was not the true religion either; therefore he left it and went to the faith of the Anabaptists, adopted this, and held it to be the best religion."

26 H. Q. Janssen, *De Kerkhervorming in Vlaanderen*, II, p. 279.

27 At Ghent the religious peace was proclaimed on December 16, 1578. The regulation referred to here is contained in Article XV and reads: "In order to carry out all prescriptions mentioned above in safety and order, there shall be installed eight prominent persons, honest, respectable, and peaceful, by the councilors of both benches and both deans of the city, four of each religion, who shall have the authority to enforce these regulations and to hear questions and complaints from both sides, as well as to mediate and pacify; if necessary they shall refer such questions and complaints to the Council."

ing for the normal exercise of their religion.[28] This request placed the Calvinistic authorities before the development they had feared and obliged them to carry out the provisions of the 1581 synodal resolution.

The way in which this was done was, however, not what might have been expected. The "public debate" which the resolution had called for became a debate before the City Council behind closed doors, which was held on February 24, 1582. The reason for this modification of the original provision is not clear, but presumably the intention was to give the debate a minimum of publicity in order to prevent the Mennonites from obtaining any propagandistic advantage. The pretext for this privacy was probably the local character of the incident, especially the fact that it involved a request to the City Council itself. As a result of this procedure very little became known about the discussions. The chronicler de Jonghe, the only one to report on the event, informs us only that there was considerable debate about the doctrine of the Incarnation between "four ministers [Calvinists] and four or five Anabaptists." From a statement of this kind no important conclusions can be drawn. It indicates only that the two parties had numerically equal representation, and that the debate was primarily theological. Nothing can be concluded about the strength of the two churches nor about the identity of the participants. Presumably the Council awaited the end of the discussions before deliberating on the Mennonite request for the right to meet.

It is certain that Petrus Dathenus was not present; he had been living in the Palatinate since 1579 and did not return to Flanders until 1583.[29] It is probable that Jacobus Regius was a participant. Prominent in Calvinistic circles in Ghent, a well-trained theologian, Regius was also somewhat of an anti-Anabaptist specialist. The other participants were presumably ministers of the churches in Ghent or the surrounding countryside.

It is still more difficult to establish who might have been the Mennonite participants in the debate. Only one relatively certain surmise may be hazarded; namely, that there was no qualified minister from within the Ghent congregation itself. In the same year a minister at Antwerp, Albrecht Verspeck, had promised at Amsterdam to visit Ghent every four months to carry out the duties of a minister there.[30] It may be assumed that the Mennonites, aware of the importance of making a good showing in this debate, called on the best of their leaders, especially those ac-

28 De Jonghe, *op. cit.*, II, p. 279; W. te Water, *Historie der Hervormde Kerk te Gent* (Utrecht, 1756), p. 83.

29 Tho Ruys, *Petrus Dathenus* (Utrecht, 1919), pp. 156-82. B. ten Cate, *op. cit.*, II, pp. 215 f.

30 Vos, *DtA*, p. 260; the representatives of the congregation at Ghent were also present at this meeting.

quainted with the Ghent congregation. Pauwels van Meenen, for instance, was a faithful visitor of the church there. He was there in 1581 to baptize Cattelyne van Hulle, and shortly afterward to perform her marriage.[31] Hans Busschaert as well had held well-attended meetings in Ghent in 1581.[32] Other ministers may well have been sent from Antwerp, but we know too little to hazard a guess at their identity.

Although de Jonghe says nothing more, there can be no doubt of the outcome of the debate. It is unthinkable that the Calvinists in power should have made the slightest concessions to the Mennonites. Their decision was certainly of a piece with the hostility shown by the same authorities in the following year. In May, 1583, it was announced that all citizens must declare under oath that they considered Philip II as having been dethroned. The performance of such an oath was, of course, inadmissible for the Mennonites. Lieven Tobast was summoned to appear before the Ghent Council for his refusal to obey the command. Asked whether he had reconsidered his position, he answered that he could not change his attitude, and added that in his part of the city there were many others of similar convictions. Immediately Lieven Tobast was banished for life. The same sentence was pronounced against Vincent Roose, also for refusal to take the oath of loyalty to the new regime.[33] Only a few months later Fierin Grysperre, an overly active dissenter, who had announced his meetings by distributing notices throughout the city, was also permanently banished from the city.[34]

These arrests and sentences as well as the debate were typical of the attitude taken toward Mennonitism by the Calvinists at the height of their power. They indicate that the brotherhood, even though enjoying greater numerical strength compared to official confessions, continued to suffer under severe limitations of freedom. Practically, the Mennonites had been tolerated since 1576 only in so far as their convictions and their claims did not conflict with the Calvinistic regime. Although conditions were improved, the conflict had not reached a peaceful resolution. This perhaps explains in part their ability to resist restored Catholicism in the last years of the sixteenth and the first quarter of the seventeenth century.[35]

---

31 Ghent City, *Crime*, 1591-94, fol. 58vo.

32 *Ibid.*, 1581-83, cover.   33 *Ibid.*, fol. 11.   34 *Ibid.*, fol. 172.

35 Willem van Ameys, bailiff of Courtrai, was summoned to explain why he had not prevented a meeting of Mennonites. (Ghent State, *RVSC*, 1581-85, fol. 49-57vo.) The attitude of the Calvinists toward Lutherans was likewise not tolerant. Zegher Conincxberghe, a Lutheran minister, was charged by the Lutheran congregation at Antwerp to hold meetings at Ghent. As soon as his presence in Ghent came to light, he was called before the authorities. He was told to leave Ghent immediately, and threatened with serious punishment if he did not comply, (Ghent City, *Crime*, 1573-74, fol. 173vo-174.)

IV. THE PERIOD OF
GRADUAL EMIGRATION: 1586-c.1640

Under the capable leadership of Alessandro Farnese the restoration of the Spanish regime did not follow the pattern of Alva's terrorism. First of all, a change was noticeable in military methods. On their campaign through Southern Flanders the soldiers were no longer allowed to sack the conquered cities. In the peace negotiations as well the new governor showed deep diplomatic insight, and his religious policy was just as adroit. He controlled the activity of the new Great Inquisitor, Pieter de Backere, just as he had formerly kept the army within bounds.

The Acts of Surrender, *e.g.*, those of the city of Ghent (September 17, 1584), show the new governor's intent to follow a clearly conceived policy. The Catholic magistrates were to be bound to apply Article IV, which read: "And to show that we do not desire to destroy or depopulate said city, His Highness will be satisfied if aforesaid freemen, citizens, and inhabitants are allowed to continue to have their residence and living quarters for the period of two years, without being subject to investigation, on condition that they are not rebellious, scandalous, or offensive; in the meantime counseling and deciding whether they wish to conform to the practices of the Holy, Ancient, Catholic, Apostolic and Roman religion, or if not, they will be free to leave the country whenever they wish within said two years. In that case they will be allowed the free and complete use of all their goods, to dispose of them, to transport, sell, or destroy them, as they wish, or to choose and appoint someone to hold and administer them."[1] Severe, in that henceforth no dissent was to be tolerated, and at the same time moderate, in the provision of a two-year period for adjustment, these treaties represent a departure from all former methods of struggle. At the same time the goal remains the same: the removal of all signs of Protestant activity from the king's Netherlands.

Soon enough the authorities were to observe on the part of the Mennonites a complete indifference to the measures taken against Protestantism. At least in the large cities, the Mennonites were behaving as if there

1 De Jonghe, *op. cit.*, II, p. 448.

were no prohibition of preaching and other activities and as if no changes at all had been made. On March 17, 1585, hardly six months after the ratification of the Reconciliation Act, the magistrates of Ghent arrested nine Mennonites just as they had assembled at the home of Jan de Cleercq to collect contributions and prepare for the distribution of these relief funds to the poor of their congregation.[2] Those arrested were Pieter Haesbaert, Jacques de Cleercq, Jacob de Joncheere, Bauwens Tyncke, Joos Bouckaert, Pieter Tryon, Jan de Backere, Manasses de Bats, and Jacques Houtermans. The first of these told his judges forthrightly that the meetings of the brotherhood had never been interrupted and that these meetings were held sometimes inside the city, sometimes outside.

It was clear to the authorities that since the brethren had been caught red-handed in an illicit assembly a penalty was required. Yet the Ghent Council hesitated to take measures on its own initiative, and first asked the Council of Flanders for instructions concerning two questions.[3] First, was Ghent authorized to hold the nine Mennonites in prison and begin proceedings against them? Secondly, were they authorized to act against all the numerous Mennonites resident in the city, who were still making new converts?

The Council of Flanders cautiously declared itself incompetent to give advice to Ghent's emissaries. In view of the exceptional circumstances prevailing in the months just following the Reconciliation Act, the Council, however, ventured an advisory opinion on the first question. It favored immediate prosecution of the prisoners for violation of Farnese's orders, but refused to commit itself on the second count, recommending that it be brought to the governor himself.

On March 26, 1585, the three emissaries, Pieter de Vos, Philippus Lenorman, and Franchois de Groote, were summoned the second time by the Ghent Council to the Council of Flanders.[4] During this audience it was decided that the nine Mennonites should be punished at least with banishment. Since, however, neither the city nor the provincial authorities were willing to take the responsibility for this decision it was agreed to ask Farnese's approval. Because of the undiminished activity of the Mennonites at Ghent, the Council of Flanders further recommended a thorough investigation of the religious convictions of the citizenry, as well

---

2 Ghent State, *RVSC*, 1585-86, fol. 1 ff. Also *Series K, Register van Criminele sententien,* 1585-1641, fol. 1 ff.

3 Ghent State, *Oudburg*, No. 161, fol. 149vo. "Besides it was announced that the bailiff had apprehended some heretical persons. Not knowing too well what to do with them, and after having asked several persons, clergy and others, it is now resolved to ask advice of Milords the Council."

4 Ghent State, *RVSC*, 1585-86, fol. 3.

as the institution of an obligatory loyalty oath. In a missive of April 10, 1585, the city fathers informed Alessandro Farnese as to how they had dealt with their prisoners and asked his advice. On the same occasion they asked whether Article IV of the Reconciliation Act was applicable to "Anabaptists."[5]

A letter of the Secret Council dated May 13, 1585, said that Farnese had informed the Secret Council of his opinion concerning the Ghent Mennonites in a private letter (which has not been preserved) dated May 2. The governor desired the punishment of the prisoners, leaving the fixing of the sentence to the Council of Flanders as supreme judicial authority, and further suggested that Pieter Haesbaert and his fellow prisoners be submitted to further interrogation to gather information concerning the activity of the brotherhood in Ghent.[6] Farnese left no doubt that he desired no exceptional measures against the Mennonites. "There is no reason," he declared, "to maintain that the Anabaptists are less covered by the terms of the present [treaty] than are the Calvinists or other sectarians, who are no less pernicious; yea who are more seditious, violent, turbulent, and dangerous than are said Anabaptists."

It was very normal for the governor to express himself in this way. The Ghent authorities considered the problem of dissent from a local viewpoint and judged that most resistance came from the Mennonites. Alessandro Farnese had the broader view and knew that a revival of Calvinistic agitation would bring with it much greater dangers; the case of the Calvinists at Bruges, with which we shall soon deal, had been instructive for him in this respect.

The Secret Council accepted the governor's suggestions in full and repeated to him the proposal of the Council of Flanders, that another loyalty oath be required of the population.[7] Now the fate of the prisoners could be quickly determined. The Council of Flanders having requested fifty-year banishment, without confiscation of goods, in its letters of September 16[8] and 18,[9] this sentence was pronounced by the Ghent magis-

---

5 Ghent State, *Series 94 bis*, dossier No. 22. This letter was delivered to the Court at Brussels by Maillaert de Vuldere, Pensioner, and Ghyselbrecht Cortewille. (Ghent City, *Stadsrekeningen*, 1584-85, fol. 368.)

6 Farnese's order was executed faithfully. On June 7, 1585, Groote, pensioner of Ghent, was instructed by the Council of Flanders to urge the city fathers to ascertain "who is their minister, their administrator of alms or other matters, where and how often they have been meeting, who else has been present, furthermore all those who are of their faith, as well as those who give and receive the alms . . ." (Ghent State, *RV Series K*, fol. 3).

7 Brussels Royal, *Geheime Raad (Spaansch bewind)*, dossier No. 1,117.

8 Ghent State, *RVSC*, 1585-86, fol. 38vo.

9 *Ibid.*, fol. 40vo.

trate on September 20.[10] The fact that the deliberations on this case had taken more than six months demonstrates the serious difficulties that arose from the arrest of non-Catholics during the two-year religious "cooling-off period." Even in 1586 the bailiff of den Oudburg thought it wise to refer some Protestants to the Council of Flanders before condemning them, since "he didn't know too well what to do with these people."

The Ghent government was not the only one to find that the clandestine organization of the Mennonites was still functioning. In Bruges, which had surrendered to the Spanish on May 20, 1584, the same observation was made. Here, however, the Mennonites were working under entirely different circumstances, since they were not alone in their opposition to the Catholics. During the winter of 1584-85, the Calvinists, convinced that Spain could make no claim to a final victory as long as Ghent had not fallen, had accomplished an impressive regrouping of their forces.[11] They looked for help from the North, from the reserve troops of Maurice of Nassau. Accordingly the Calvinists also bore the brunt of the repression following the indiscretions of a thirteen-year-old boy who had betrayed their plans. The Catholic government had its hands full with this new attempt of the Calvinists to gain ground. Between 1584 and 1587 over one hundred sentences of expulsion were pronounced against Calvinists. It is consequently not surprising that little notice was given to the capture of two Mennonites, Jan van Metminne of Cologne, and Aernout Soen of Courtrai.[12] The former admitted that the youngest of his four children had not been baptized, and refused to take his turn in serving in the civil guard, in line with the Mennonite position as defined in Wismar in August, 1555. Jan van Metminne resisted all pressure to get him to change his mind, and was consequently given three days to leave the city "forever."

Aernout Soen was no less troublesome. Originally from Courtrai, having belonged for some time to the brotherhood at Antwerp, he had settled in Bruges in 1581. He had not had his three-year-old child baptized, and refused to change his mind. He was given twenty-four hours to reconsider, facing the threat of a fifty-guilder fine and further persecution. On the following day, still refusing to yield, he was required to confess his guilt publicly and pay the fine; meanwhile someone had been sent to get the child from Soen's house and take it to the church.

10 Ghent City, *Crime*, 1585-88, fol. 7vo-8.

11 Cf. E. J. Strubbe, "Het verval van het Protestantisme te Brugge na 1584." *Annales de la Societé d'Emulation de Bruges*, 1924.

12 *Loc. cit.*, p. 18, note 5; also Bruges State, *Découvertes*, 203bis, fol. 123.

In contrast with the larger centers of population, it was impossible for the Mennonites to remain in the smaller towns. Anyone who desired to be further useful to the church, or anyone who feared persecution because he had been too visibly active, sought safety in the cities. Joost Bostijn of Courtrai was one such person. As long as possible he had remained in the city of his birth; in 1585, however, he had to leave for Bruges, where he offered his services to the local congregation.[13] The case of the nine Mennonite prisoners at Ghent was similar. None of them were of local origin; all had left their original scenes of activity in order to serve the church where its existence was still considered possible.

The situation in the interim 1585-87 was difficult; but after the expiration of this period continued activity became fully impossible. A veritable man hunt was made for the remaining leaders of the brotherhood. These leaders knew that they were especially sought and that if caught they faced certain death. This was characteristic of the repression now beginning. The leaders were killed in the least spectacular way possible—no longer burned at the stake—but the authorities were relatively mild in their treatment of ordinary members, even if they stubbornly stuck to their faith.

The archival records of the last days of Mennonitism as preserved in Bruges, Brussels, and especially in Ghent,[14] deserve special attention for their witness to the sacrificial efforts of the brethren to keep their church alive.

On December 12, 1587, Jooris de Rieu of Halewijn appeared before the Ghent authorities.[15] He had become acquainted with the brethren in Ghent, and had become an active participant in their work. The court instructed the clergy to examine him. In spite of their numerous shrewd questions he held to his convictions and the clergy recommended lifelong banishment. Sentence was pronounced accordingly on December 12; Jooris de Rieu was led to the city gates and given three days to leave Flanders, three weeks to leave the Netherlands.

Hardly a year later the city fathers discovered to their surprise that the brotherhood was still alive and strong. A man and his wife, whose names are not recorded, were arrested about January 10, 1589.[16] The woman testified that she had been baptized only three months before somewhere in the fields around Ghent. Further she told the judges, with-

13 Ibid., Découvertes, 203, fol. 135vo.

14 Aside from Ghent and Bruges, van Braght's only entry for Flanders in this period is the burning of Christiaen de Rijke at Hondschoote in December, 1588. (Van Braght, Mirror, II, p. 757.)

15 Ghent City, Crime, 1585-88, fol. 34.

16 Ghent City, Series 94 bis, dossier No. 22.

out betraying any details as to place or attendance, that she had shortly before attended a meeting in the city itself.

In the meantime the home of the arrested couple was searched. Large quantities of meat and bread, as well as a "book containing the distribution of alms or support among those of their sect," were found. After the discovery of these stores the Ghent Council wrote to Farnese on January 12: "Therefore we find the matter somewhat delicate, for the times are still so confused." The Southern Netherlands were at this time economically disabled. The emigrant van Meteren pictured the situation in perhaps too dark colors when he gave the following description: "The hunger there is so great this year (1587) . . . that substantial, stately, respectable people, splendidly dressed, in Antwerp, Brussels, Ghent, Bruges, and other cities, have been begging for bread in the evening when it was dark and they could not be recognized. Rich people dressed in velvet and silk begged for bread and sold their jewelry, furniture, and other belongings to buy bread. In the dirt of the dumping places along the street they looked for bones, turnip peels, and anything edible; they even picked up and ate a dead dog at Bruges. The wheat prices are higher than ever heard of before. The famine was less severe the next year (1588), since the fields were well taken care of and the population had decreased."[17] Discounting possible exaggerations of this emigrant historian, his description testifies nonetheless to the great poverty of the people. The discovery that these two Mennonites had in their possession considerable amounts of scarce food is proof of the prosperity of some members of the congregation; their liberality in sharing is likewise evidence of the sense of unity which bound the brethren together. Indirectly the Councilmen expressed their respect for the welfare work of the brethren, when they expressed their disinclination to act harshly: "So that we thus are concerned about how we should treat these sectarians."[18]

Such considerations bore no weight, however, in higher government circles. On the contrary, these deacons were regarded as the most dangerous and the most influential elements of the brotherhood, and logically so. The deacons were the ones who, besides their social work, informed the brethren of the meetings, who lodged the teacher and brought him to his destination, and who often preached themselves. As deacon-teachers

17 E. van Meteren, *Historie der Nederlandscer . . . oorlogene ende geschiedenissen* (2nd ed., Gorinchem, 1748-63), V, pp. 42 f.

18 The Council's message alludes to the execution of a Mennonite preacher at Hondschoote, whose double offense was having baptized and having returned to the South without the authorization of the Spanish. (Cf. note 14 above.) François de Potter, *Petit Cartulaire de Gand* (Ghent, 1885), February 7, 1589.

they were in fact the responsible ministers of the last Mennonite groups on Flemish soil.

The judges showed their understanding of the importance of the deacons in the course of the trial of Michiel Buesse and Joos de Tollenaere.[19] Both had belonged to the brotherhood for some time, having experienced the times of relative freedom. After the Catholic victory they had not ceased their work. The restrictive measures against all Protestants which began to be applied in 1587 after the expiration of the interim did not frighten them. Hans Busschaert visited repeatedly in their homes in 1587 and 1588. The two men were responsible for his safety. They were the ones who found places, within or without the city, where the faithful could be strengthened by the eloquent preaching of their beloved teacher, and where new members of the group could be baptized. Buesse and Tollenaere also took the risks involved in collecting money and gifts in kind for the needy of the congregation. Rightly the verdict of April 13, 1589, called them "the main pillars among the brethren of your congregation." After death by strangling inside the count's castle in order to avoid the sensation of a public execution, their bodies were hanged outside the citadel.

The same day a Mennonite woman, Joosijne Swijnts, met the same fate.[20] She had been baptized just seven months before by Hans Busschaert. The charge against her consisted only of having been rebaptized and attending several meetings, yet we believe that her activities were more far-reaching and that she had a more important function than that of a mere member. For on May 9 Tannekin van de Zande was condemned only to exile, on a charge much more serious than the one cited against Joosijne Swijnts.[21] Tannekin had been baptized by Hans Busschaert at Ghent, not seven months but thirteen years previously. She had never left the city and during all those years she had been a faithful attendant at all the Mennonite meetings within and without the city. When arrested, she refused to betray any of her fellow believers and avoided every trap by declaring that "most of them have left the city." Just as stubbornly she clung to her faith in the face of efforts to lead her to recant. Nevertheless she escaped the death penalty. This is due probably to the fact that she had never been more than an ordinary member, whereas Joosijne had borne great responsibilities.

Eighteen months later, on November 9, 1590, Geeraert van de Walle

---

19 Ghent City, *Crime*, 1588-91, fol. 19 f.

20 *Ibid.*, fol. 19vof.

21 *Ibid.*, fol. 20vo.

of Hansbeke appeared for trial at Ghent.[22] He was a simple workingman, who sometimes supplemented his income by making brooms for farmers and who by his own study had learned to read very well and to write a little. During the trial he stood his ground, answering in a clever, even a mocking way the judges' shrewdest questions. Van de Walle recounted that he had belonged to the Mennonite fellowship since 1578. Since the requirements for admission were very high, he had not been baptized until 1587, by Hans Busschaert at Vlissingen. Asked by his judge for more details about the baptismal ceremony and those baptized with him, Geeraert complained of a bad memory and said that he could recall only that "there had been more than two or three." When the questions concerned him more personally he was again able to answer. He had returned to Flanders from Vlissingen two years before. He had stayed with his uncle Willem van de Walle at Hansbeke, later with Karel Verplaetzen at Nevele; now in Ghent he had been living with a weaver, Joos Boethals, and sometimes with his cousin Karel Steyaert. Geeraert must have known when he named these friends that they were already in security. The criminal files show that none of them were persecuted. He betrayed little about the meeting he had attended six days earlier in the city. He would say only that at a certain time he was in a weaver's workshop where some girls were spinning, and that after him several other people from inside and outside the city also entered; one of this group had led the meeting. He avoided answering the question whether he himself had taught at this meeting by asking the judge whether in his opinion this would not have been for the benefit of those in attendance. Further asked whether he was a "teacher," he admitted having spoken a few times at Hansbeke, but said that otherwise he "only desired to hear and to learn to the best of his capacity and knowledge." The only correspondence with Zeeland which he would admit carrying on was with his own parents. Asked whether he would again use the New Testament which had been taken from him if it were returned to him, he answered sarcastically, "That's what it's made for."

It is very strange that nothing more is registered in the criminal records about Geeraert van de Walle. Logically he should have been condemned to death after this confession, but no sentence can be found in the archives. Nor are there any traces of the further fate of the Mennonite Wouters Wychelssone, who was arrested at Sint-Winnoxbergen in May, 1591.[23] We are better informed about the last three Mennonites who

22 *Ibid.*, fol. 83vo.
23 Ghent State, *RVBW*, reg. 63, fol. 107.

8

came up for trial in the 1590's: Reineux Pantens, Cattelyne van Hulle, and Michiel de Cleercq.

Reineux Pantens was tried on June 30, 1592.[24] He was forty-eight years old, a native of Roeselaere. Sought by the Ghent police since 1577, he had escaped by continually changing his residence. At the time of his arrest he was living with Jan Doverdaghe. He had remained active after the expiration of the interim of 1585-87, and had even succeeded in purchasing exemption from guard duty. He refused obstinately to give information about Mennonite meetings, asking the Council whether they considered it a "meeting" when "three or four of them had walked together." The interrogators were more successful with his twelve-year-old daughter, who was brought into the courtroom after he was led out. Intimidated by the proceedings in the impressive "castle" (which in modern times is the post office), Lyntken in her innocence revealed many details which her parents would never have betrayed under the worst torture.[25] She related that her father had most to do with Dierick de Schryvere, Jan Stamp, and the sisters Adriaeneken and Tanneken Kiekepost. All these people met at her father's room at least every Sunday at two o'clock, when her father or sometimes Stamp read "something from several books." She reported that the parents of the Kiekepost sisters disapproved of their Mennonite sympathies and had repeatedly asked them to return to the Catholic Church. Recently Pantens had been having difficulties with Jan Doverdaghe, his Catholic landlord, because of these meetings, but thus far he had been able to avoid being evicted.

Lyntken suddenly became very careful when asked who was the owner of the money which had been found in a trunk in her father's room, and whether it was to be used for the support of the poor members of the congregation. First she replied that "she would not answer that question, neither would she name the owner." Under further pressure her answers were vague. She thought the givers must have been Franchois and Jan; she did not remember their full names. They lived somewhere "outside the Keyser Gate, without knowing exactly their residence or last name."

Lyntken was led on to describe a typical country meeting. With her father, Jan Stamp, and Dierick de Schryvere she had recently gone for a walk. Once they were outside the Keyser Gate, she noticed that they had been joined by several "country folk whom she does not know." Suddenly they stopped walking and seated themselves behind a hillock. Here,

---

24 Ghent City, *Crime*, 1591-94, fol. 52 f.
25 *Ibid.*, fol. 53vo-55.

in the open air and far from all indiscreet observers, her father and Jan Stamp spoke after the reading of a passage of Scripture. This was followed by a discussion on the same subject in which everyone present participated.

The Council was fortunate to have obtained some information from this child, for her father would reveal nothing. Again and again Reineux Pantens was dragged to the rack, but he never betrayed any of the brethren. He incriminated only himself by the admission that he had done everything within his power to prevent the goods of refugees from coming into the hands of the authorities. He helped his fellow believers to escape and took care of their property for them as well.[26] The standard sentence for Mennonite leaders, death by strangling within the count's castle, followed by public hanging of the corpse, was pronounced on September 15, 1592.[27]

Another prominent figure from this period was Michiel de Cleercq, whose activities we have already traced until 1588. After this date he became more active, together with Reineux Pantens. Michiel took care of the poor in addition to his preaching. He collected money and gifts in kind, and took the risk of hiding in his room part of the collected goods. The day before his arrest, June 29, he had hauled three heavy sacks of food to his home with the assistance of a woman whose name he refused to disclose in spite of torture. He had gone to bed after the day's hard work, when he was aroused by hammering on his door. His attempt to escape by the window was futile, for the house was surrounded.

Michiel stood firm to the end. However sorely he was tried, not a single incautious word passed his lips. The only Mennonite he named was one Franchois Hubrecht surnamed Lochtentier, a yarn merchant. This revelation was, however, of no importance, since de Cleercq refused to indicate Hubrecht's place of residence. Rightly judged to be one of the pillars of the brethren, he died on the same day the same death as Reineux Pantens,[28] September 15, 1592. He was the last Mennonite martyr in Flanders, indeed in the entire Netherlands.

The authorities were less severe with Cattelyne van Hulle, Dierick de Schryvere, and Jan Stamp.[29] Cattelyne had been baptized at Ghent by Pauwels van Meenen in 1581 and had made the acquaintance of Jacob Martens, one of the brethren, whom she later married. The mother of four children, she was not spared many trials. During the siege of the city

26 *Ibid.*, fol. 58vo-60.
27 *Ibid.*, fol. 72vof.
28 *Ibid.*, fol. 55vo-57vo, **72vof.**
29 *Ibid.*, 55vof., 58vof.

by Farnese's armies her husband and second-youngest child died; hardly two years later the youngest died. None of this kept her from being faithful in attending meetings outside the St. Baafs Gate, where Hans Busschaert preached. Arrested, she remained true to her convictions. Her goods were confiscated and she was condemned to "eternal" exile, under the threat of hanging should she return.[30]

Dierick de Schryvere, who undoubtedly had been a member of the brotherhood for a long time, since his home served as a collection center for gifts for the poor of the church, and Jan Stamp, who had often spoken in meetings, were less steadfast. Their conviction weakened before the first test. Already on July 1, 1592, the day after their arrest, they were released on condition that they report to the authorities whenever summoned.

The trials thus far described show that during the period 1587-92 Mennonitism had not ceased to struggle with all the means remaining at its disposal. Meetings in limited groups within the city, larger meetings outside the city walls, collections in favor of the less fortunate in the congregation—all this went on as usual. Those responsible, the deacon-teachers, fulfilled their task well. They were also the best qualified persons to take care of the interests of those who were forced to flee, since they were most closely in touch with the Mennonites in Holland and Zeeland, where a large number of Flemish refugees had already resettled.

Probably Hans Busschaert was the most effective liaison agent between the Northern and Southern Netherlands. Flemish himself, very well acquainted with the Northern Netherlands, especially with Zeeland, where he is reported to have baptized in 1587, Busschaert never abandoned the sorely tried brethren in his native province. Repeatedly his presence was reported to the authorities, but always too late.[31] Busschaert knew better than anyone else the needs of the Flemish Mennonites. Despite the lack of formal proof it is indubitable that he told about these needs in emigrant circles in the North. His appeal did not go unheard. In 1589 Joos de Tollenaere received the sum of one hundred guilders from the congregation at Haarlem to be used for the support of the poor;[32] Zeeland as well did not fail to help when needed.

In 1592, when the known leaders were executed, this assistance from the North was probably instrumental in preventing the almost inevitable disappearance of Flemish Mennonitism. Soon signs of revival could again

30 If van Braght's report of a "Kalleken N.," who was released only after recanting, refers to this same Cattelyne, van Braght was misinformed.
31 Ghent City, *Crime*, 1588-91, fol. 83.
32 Van Braght, *Mirror*, II, pp. 764-766.

be seen in some of the traditional Mennonite centers. Joost Bostijn was called before the Bruges Council in 1593, and confessed having maintained contacts with Mennonites in the city.[33]

At Ghent, Janneken de Meyere declared to the authorities on August 21, 1598, "that they should not have arrested her, for there were at least one thousand male Protestants in the city."[34] This figure is certainly exaggerated; had there been one thousand Protestants in the city there would have been other signs of their presence. Nonetheless, the statement attests to the continued existence of Protestant groups, just as there is no reason to doubt the existence of Mennonites, even though the documentary traces of their presence grow more and more rare. In 1605 Robert Robbertsz addressed an appeal "to the congregation of God in Holland, Zeeland, Friesland, Flanders, Brabant, and the other provinces; whom he warns against the false prophets such as the Jesuit Costerus and his like."[35] In 1606 Paschasius Schelstratius, the priest of the Saint Anna parish in Ghent, reported that he had administered Catholic baptism to one Petronella, whose parents had come from Holland or Zeeland, perhaps as returning Flemish Mennonite refugees; the child had been left unbaptized until the age of nine.[36]

Three years later information was received at Brussels of frequent large Mennonite meetings in and around Lovendegem. The Mennonites felt relatively secure, thanks to the presence in their midst of the Council member Cornelis Arents, who had long been a sympathizer.[37] In recent weeks, according to the message sent to Archduke Albrecht on November 7, 1609, a teacher from the Haarlem congregation had been present. The archduke reacted by ordering all civil authorities to renew the proclamation of the edict against the "rebaptizers."

At a meeting of Catholic bishops held at Mechelen in 1617 it was noted that Mennonitism still existed in the southern provinces, and the decision to combat it mercilessly was renewed.[38] In 1630, responding to news of Mennonite activity continuing around Lovendegem and Zomergem, the Council of Flanders ordered an investigation throughout the

33 Bruges State, *Découvertes*, 203, fol. 135vo.

34 Ghent City, *Register Crimineel*, 1593-99, fol. 5vo, 127vo.

35 Meulman Collection, No. 1,035.

36 Bruges City, *Clergé séculier et régulier*, 1428-1700, loose item, 1606.

37 Ghent City, *Culte et Bienfaisance*, reg. 15. Gaillard, *Correspondance de Philippe II*, pp. 448 f. Council member Cornelis Arents was summoned by the court and confessed to having attended a Mennonite meeting. He was fined thirty carolus-guilders and ordered to attend mass regularly and go to confession at the set dates.

38 Ghent City, *Acta et Resoluta congregatione episcoporum provinciale Mechliniensis*, 1617.

entire country.[39] This measure resulted in the arrest of Samuel Pits and his seventy-three-year-old mother, Lady Maria de Provin, both of whom were induced to talk.[40] They revealed that a prospering congregation, already several years old, existed in the area. The brethren were mostly rich merchants, who frequently visited the Aardenburg market. When in Aardenburg they never failed to attend meetings held at a place called "ten Biezen."[41] For a long time the congregation at Lovendegem had held its meetings in an attic. By 1629, when the group had become too large for the room, it was decided to furnish a house for the meetings. Before long this building was found to be too small, and a second was built. The financial resources of this congregation must have been exceptional.[42] In addition to their buildings they supported a minister whom they called from their midst, Jacob van Maldegem, born at Zomergem (or Hansbeke?), who had grown up among the Flemish. He had seen the birth and growth of the group at Lovendegem and had probably had a large part in urging the scattered Mennonites in Flanders to regroup themselves and to establish this new congregation.

The churches in Zeeland followed this new development with interest. Direct contacts could be made at Aardenburg on market days, at

39 *Message des Sciences* (Ghent, 1886), pp. 232-38. Ghent State, *RVBW*, reg. 140. Ghent City, *Varia D*, No. 1,088.

40 Maria de Provin or van Provijn was the daughter of Master Lieven van Provijn, "Lord of the Highways, High Alderman of the Land of Waes and member of the Council of Flanders," and of Lady Elizabeth Ophoge. During her trial she named the books which were her customary reading matter: Says on the 15th that she brought most of these books from Holland, where she bought part of them; the rest she received from her husband (who belonged to the same sect) and these are the books: the New Testament printed at Amsterdam, anno 1610, together with the Psalms of David, translated by Pieter Dathenus, bound together with a catechism with red copper mounting; the Bible printed in 1564 in large octavo; another New Testament printed in 1563 in 16mo; another New Testament in small 16mo; a book beginning "eene weemoedige ende Christelycke onschuldygynge, etc.," by Menno Simons, printed in 1576, together with some other tracts by the same author in small octavo; *Enchiridion oft Hantboecxken*, by Dirk Philips, printed in 1564 in 16mo, which explains the faith of the defendant; the *IJe Liedebouck*, printed at Amsterdam in 1583 in 16mo; *een vredige verantwoordinghe*, by Cornelis de Cuuper, in octavo; *de Boom des wetens* in small octavo; *Triumphus Cupidinis*, printed in Antwerp, 1628; *een handtboucken*, printed at 's Hertoghenbosch, 1610 autore verepeo in 16mo; *Historien Justini*, printed at Arnhem in 1610; *Disputatie van Antechrist*, by Pater Heffius, in 12mo; *Het lusthofken van onse lieve vrauwe*, printed at Louvain in 1620 in 16mo; *de naervolgynghe Christi* without beginning, in 16mo. (Brussels Royal, *Conseil Privé Espagnol*, dossier No. 1,117, Nov. 27, 1629.)

41 H. Broex van Groenen wrote as early as 1864: ". . . there were still Mennonites living who remained secretly faithful to their religion, but because public confession was too dangerous they crossed the border near Aardenburg to meet in faith with the brethren and sisters there." ("Uit het verleden der Doopsgezinde gemeente te Aardenburg," in *Doopsgezinde Bijdragen*, IV [1864], p. 85.)

42 Ghent City, *Varia D*, No. 1,088, fol. 3: "Nevertheless the number of said Anabaptists has grown and is still growing daily, because most of them are very wealthy." Concerning the Pits case cf. Brussels Royal, *Conseil Privé Espagnol*, No. 1,107.

which time money gifts could be sent. An elder from Zeeland visited Lovendegem twice a year to baptize new converts; he also brought clothing for the poor in the congregation.[43]

As alert as the "Government of the Counterreformation" was, it was unable to check this development because of the impossibilty of checking the movement of merchants. Even in 1630, after the arrest of Samuel Pits and his mother had given them abundant new information, the police were unable to capture anyone else. The members of the church either had left the country or were hiding under a safe pseudonym. Thus the Council of Flanders was unable to affirm to the Secret Council that the Lovendegem area had been purified of the heresy.

The Council expressed the opinion that it was not sufficient to require that everyone attend the parish church. Many, it was feared, could perform this *acte de presence* and remain free, as soon as the occasion should allow, to give expression to their true Mennonite convictions. The fear, implicit in this warning, that Mennonitism might yet find a new lease on life, was unfounded; and yet clandestine small groups continued to exist through the 1630's. About 1636 a wealthy cloth-merchant, Christiaen van Eeghem, was obliged to leave his home at Lichtervelde. He and his son Jacob were to become pillars of the Aardenburg congregation.[44] Christiaen's nephew, Adriaan van Eeghem, was a teacher or elder in Middelburg from 1655 to 1709.[45] Adriaan was born of Roman Catholic parents at Kortemark, four miles southwest of Torhout, in 1631. His parents were considered to be good Catholics, and he served for some time as a choirboy; yet they were part of a small group of Mennonite emigrants who fled to the North in 1639 or 1640. The fact that in the late 1630's new converts were still being made is a substantial guarantee that Mennonitism was still very much alive. Furthermore, there is no clear reason to regard this known migration of 1639-40 as the last. It would be premature to attempt to fix an exact date for the final disappearance of Mennonitism in Flanders.

It is easy to see why the migrations, individual and collective, from Flanders to the North generally went in the direction of Aardenburg. Jacob van Maldegem, already named as the founder of the Lovendegem-Zomergem congregation, was also the father of the Aardenburg group. Aardenburg and Sluis had been occupied in the name of the Northern Netherlands by Maurice of Orange, who did not legally recognize the

---

43 Ghent City, *Varia D*, No. 1,088, fol. 16vo.

44 Christian Peter van Eeghem Jr., *Adriaan van Eeghem, doopsgezinde leerar te Middelburg, Eene Historische Studie* (Amsterdam, 1886), p. 7.

45 *Ibid.*, pp. 1-9.

Mennonites but at least did not disturb them. Aardenburg was thus the natural place of refuge and temporary residence for emigrants until they could settle farther north in Holland.

This northward retreat concludes the last phase of the unequal battle which Flemish Mennonites sustained for over a century before finally conceding defeat before the authorities who sought their complete elimination. Their story is a moving page in the history of the Southern Netherlands Reformation. May the writing of church history henceforth give them their due!

DOCUMENTS

1. Cornelis van Valconisse, former monk, describes to the judges his journey in the Northern Netherlands, where he often stayed in Anabaptist circles.[1]

Asked whether he has heard about this sect which arose in Holland, says: When coming through Holland, he stayed in Rotterdam, near the church, in the house of a widow whose name he cannot tell, except that she did charitable work and was active among the poor. Into that house had come two men who belonged to said Anabaptist sect and went from city to city to get other people into their sect.[2] The one is from Amsterdam, but the witness does not know his name or address; as to appearance he was of average build, with broad shoulders and a heavy beard, about fifty years old. The witness cannot say how he made his living. The other was a young man of about thirty years, living at Leyden near the bridge on the right side, and his name is Jan and he sells wine in jugs, without operating a tavern.

The witness [Cornelis] says further that the next morning he and Jan had a long discussion concerning the Anabaptist sect, which was zealously supported by Jan and attacked by the witness. Jan told the witness that his wife was with child and that even if it should cost his life, he would not have the child baptized. Jan did all he could to get the witness to join said sect and told him that the members of the said sect live in community [of goods].

Further they do not believe that Jesus Christ received anything of the nature of Our Lady; that if one is born of the Spirit he can no longer sin, and that men have a free will, and other points which the witness cannot remember. Said Jan also told the witness that the same year several hundred people would go out to preach and to convert people to their sect and that they already are sending people out daily to that end. Just as Paul never rested, but went from city to city to convert the world.

Jan also told the witness that they have a way of meeting together in a certain private house, where they gather in certain rooms and read the Bible, and everyone tells what he has learned and remembers about their sect and thus they interpret the Scriptures. And because the witness refused to follow their sect and opinion, they did not allow him to associate and eat and drink with Jan and his companions, who were with him in the house (and whom the witness did not know).

Witness went from Rotterdam to Bergen op Zoom and stayed at the home of Dignus de Brauwere, who weaves wool combings and lives there near the gate leading to "ter thulste," where the following came by night to recite their lessons:

1 March 17, 1534. Brussels Royal, *Office fiscal du Brabant*, No. 1194.

2 These were presumably two of the twelve missionaries sent out from Münster by Jan Matthijsz in 1534 (*Doopsgezinde Bijdragen*, 1917, p. 98); probably one of them was Jan Beukelszoon of Leiden.

105

a peddler, Jan, living at Bergen; a cabinetmaker who is supposed to be the best artisan in Brabant, with his wife; a woman; and a silversmith from Amsterdam, named Jan—witness cannot name or describe all these people. He says that Jan from Amsterdam is one of the leaders, probably one of those of whom he heard who go from city to city, bearing their message and winning followers of the said Anabaptist sect.

All those people are badly infected by that sect and did their best to bring Cornelis to their opinion, but he did not yield. He says the reason he lodged there was that he was related to his host. And the witness heard someone say that all those people are fugitives; as for a disputation of this or any other sect, he was not present, though he has heard talk about it.

2. Andries van der Mandele and his wife testify against Cornelis de Clerc, who preached Anabaptism at Bruges after his return from Lübeck.[3]

Preparatory inquiry on the case of Cornelis de Clerc, shoemaker, and Pieter Lem, maker of fur caps.

Jozyne, wife of Andries van der Mandele, about forty-one years old, declared under oath that about five or six years ago Cornelis came to live at her home to learn the trade; as far as she knows, it was two years later, when he almost knew the trade, that he married the daughter-in-law of Lanceloot Louchier, the reclaimer of wool wastes, who was punished here as a Lutheran. He kept working with her [the witness] till half a year ago, when he went to Lübeck to meet his father-in-law, who had invited him there in the hope of getting something from him. His trip took about two months.

After his return he came to work with her again, but only for two days. Then he was dismissed because when the workmen in the shop had asked him how it was at Lübeck, he answered that there was no difference between the days any more, but they ate whatever they had, on Friday as well as on Monday, that they did not go to confession, hear the mass, nor fast. And when two friars passed by he said, "There go two wolves in men's clothing": and when they heard Crispijn, the great bell of [the church of] the Holy Saviour, ringing at noon, he said, "What do the saints have to do with bells?" Because of this the other workmen became very angry and told him that if he went on that way, they would beat him out of the shop.

He also spoke in the shop about Saint Paul and the Gospel, saying, "Here Saint Paul says thus or so." One of the workmen, who had worked for her a long time, Jacop de Trompere, said: "Away with you, chimney preacher! If you want to hear preaching, go to the church; we don't want to hear it here."

And before he had gone to Lübeck she never had seen or heard anything else about him but that he was a good Christian.

Because of all this her husband discharged him. When he spoke about Saint Paul he said that all this was in a book which Lanceloot had given him. About four days after he moved out of her house she offered to cancel the twenty-one silver guilders he owed her, if he would give her the book. But he refused and said that the book was all right, though she had wanted to have it inspected by the parish priest and return it to him if it was all right.

She declared furthermore that for a year or more she saw a man who was

---

3 February 27, 1535. Bruges State, *Crimineel Informatiebouck*, 1532-38, fol. 79 f.

said to be a glass blower, and a cutler, and a man named Pier de Clevere, coming every workday to the house of Pieter Lem. When she asked the wife of one of the neighbors why they were meeting, she had answered, "What do I know about it? They read; they use a book." And on Sundays Pieter himself went out often.

Andries van der Mandele, the shoemaker, forty years old, declared under oath that he had never noticed anything about Cornelis different from other Christians before he went to Lübeck. But about four months ago, having returned from Lübeck, and being asked by the workmen how things were there, he told them that there no one bothered to fast, to go to confession, to make a difference in food between Friday and other days, or to go to mass, except for one mass a week.

The witness had also heard him say that he too had been to confession and the Holy Sacrament, but he chattered on that he thought that the same words were often repeated; he did not know whether these were vain repetition or blasphemy or something else. For this reason the witness discharged him.

He knows nothing about Pieter Lem except that he is very quiet.

3. Sharp attacks by Cornelis de Muer against the Roman Catholic clergy and practices.[4]

Preparatory inquiry in the case of Cornelis de Muer the Younger, the carpenter.

Jan de Raemmakere, forty-one years old, declared under oath that Cornelis was under serious suspicion of Lutheranism[5] among his colleagues and by other persons and has traveled very much for at least four or five years. The witness heard Cornelis say that one should not go to confession, that the Council of Basel, when it required confession, made the greatest error ever seen, which happened only because of the covetousness of the priests. God never ordained it.

Also: "The Master should lead and the servants follow."[6]

"If I were to speak—although my time has not yet come—only those should be priests who can preach the Gospel and sing the mass; all men, women, and children should sing together in the Dutch tongue and all the other priests should be driven away." The witness once saw him read in a book and Cornelis wanted him to read it too, but the witness would hear nothing of it; Cornelis said it was about the priests. Witness also heard Cornelis de Muer the Elder say that Cornelis the Younger had once been driven from "ter Beerst" where he had worked and certain books he had had there were burned. Cornelis also often says, "We should be brethren in Christ."

Jan Inghebrave, carpenter, thirty-one years old, declared under oath that Cornelis de Muer the Younger is suspected of Lutheranism by his colleagues and that it is often held against him. Witness heard Cornelis say concerning confession: "It may be right or wrong; as far as I am concerned everyone should act

4 May 20, 1538. Bruges State, *loc. cit.*, fol. 180vof.

5 Cornelis' statements indicate that he was Anabaptist and not Lutheran. Cf. N. van der Zijpp's review of Verheyden, *Bruges*, in *MQR*, April, 1947, p. 124.

6 Translator's note: This phrase is capable of several interpretations. It might be understood as a paraphrase of Eph. 6:5, and a defense against the accusation that Anabaptism is socially revolutionary; or it might be an application of the thought of John 15:20 and I John 4:17, with "master" signifying Christ and "servant" the disciple.

according to his own understanding. The masters are first, the servants should follow." "The time has not yet come." He also often speaks about Saint Paul and argues with everyone who is not in agreement with his sect. The witness saw him in possession of a Flemish book, bound in parchment, in which he said there were many strange things. There should be no churches except parish churches, in which all the services should be in Flemish. The cloisters should be abolished since the inmates are nothing more than fattening pigs; it is not within the power of saints to cause men to suffer. When [Cornelis] last saw the witness sitting before St. Mark's, he said, "You are a shrewd villain, sitting here to rob the people. Relics and images of saints should not be worshiped; there should be no images at all."

He had also heard Cornelis de Muer the Elder say that when Cornelis the Younger had worked at "ter Beerst" for the Lords of Barvinchove, he had had to leave as he was being pursued and his books were burned.

Roege Gevaert, about thirty-six years old, declared under oath that on the day the Spaniards came into the city, Cornelis the Younger came to his house and talked much about the way they do in the East [Germany], that it was right, and the ways of the church here were wrong. He spoke of the monks saying that "the Franciscans were wheat wolves"; Cornelis had a booklet dealing with the sacraments and other matters, which he gave him to read. After Roege had read it, he gave it to Adriaen Gheeraerts, who gave it [so he said] to Pieter van der Leeve. Since he could not get it back for three months, Cornelis came to the witness to ask for the return of the booklet, saying that it was not his own and he would rather lose his life than the booklet.

4. The sufferings of Jan Styaertz and his cousin Pieter.[7]

May 20, 1538. Present: Rede and Breydel, council members.

About this year, 1538, there were in Flanders two cousins, the one named Styaertz and the other Pieter. These two young and God-seeking striplings lived with their parents in a village in Flanders named Mereedor. As they were very zealous for God and searched the Holy Scriptures they soon perceived that those who believed and were regenerated should receive Christian water baptism, as a sign of having buried their former sins and being risen with Christ and walking in newness of life. Being now desirous of baptism, they traveled into Germany to inquire after other brethren of like faith. But not finding such as they desired, they soon returned home to their parents in Flanders. There they earnestly sought the Lord their God, and gained a good reputation, doing much good to the poor, and saying with Zacchaeus that if they had defrauded anyone, they would restore it fourfold.

On observing this the blind papists, bitterly hating the light of truth, took these two young lambs out of their parents' homes in Mereedor and brought them to a village near Ghent called Vinderhout where they were cast into a miserable dungeon. Once when their sister came to bring them some good shirts, they told her that they could not protect them from the worms which were in their food, eating it, and in their clothes and on their bodies. They further said: "Here is a Bible, whose content, as well as the cause of our bondage, will yet come to light after our death."

---

7 Van Braght, *Mirror*, II, p. 44.

The said Jan Styaertz was once released from prison on account of illness, and could (it seems) have escaped; but he voluntarily returned to prison, desiring gladly to die with his dear brother for Jesus' name. Thus after a certain time they were led to the slaughter. Pieter, being first to die, lifting his eyes to heaven, called boldly to Jan Styaertz: "Fight valiantly, my dear brother; for I see the heavens open above us!" They were both put to death by the sword at Vinderhout.

Thus were these young plants in the garden of the Lord consumed and devoured by the monstrous beast that came up out of the sea. But they had no power over their immortal souls, which took their flight to God, where they shall forever live in unspeakable joy. When their parents walked from Mereedor to Vinderhout to inquire after their sons, the villagers told them that they had already been put to death by the sword. Thus they were bereft of their children by these tyrants.

5. Jan van Sol of Dordrecht appears before the Council of State with his plan for combating Anabaptism (1550).[8]

1. It should be made public at all those places where announcements usually are made that a woman who gives birth to a child must have the child baptized within twenty-four hours. If on account of some illness the child cannot live that long, it must be baptized immediately after birth, under penalty of. . . .

2. The father must accompany the child to the baptism and must ask the pastor or chaplain to give his child the sacrament of baptism and thus accept it in the fellowship of the Christian Church.

3. If the child's father is absent at the time of its birth, he must go within twenty-four hours after his return to thank the pastor or chaplain for baptizing his child and accepting it in the fellowship of the Holy Roman Church, under penalty.

(These three articles are sufficiently practicable and reasonable; still one could ask the opinion of the theologians of Louvain. Van Sol declares himself convinced of the efficacy of these articles, saying that he knows assuredly that no Anabaptist will allow his child to be baptized in infancy, nor would he be willing to bring it forward for baptism, but will let it be done, expecting to do what they will with the child later; but the foundation of their sect is that none will give his consent to baptism before the children have understanding; otherwise they are cursed and delivered to the power of the devil.

This article is practicable enough and, given the approval of Louvain, it could be restated somewhat to be legally exact.)

4. After the purification and convalescence the child's mother must go to church and as is customary stand outside until she is invited inside by the pastor or chaplain. The pastor will ask her first whether she accepts that her child has been baptized and accepted into the fellowship of the Holy Roman Church. If she agrees, she may enter the church; if not, she shall be forbidden to enter and the pastor will inform the officer, who will record the fact according to imperial command.

(To have to stand before the church is impractical and unusual; still the pastor could speak with her as the article says.)

---

[8] Brussels Royal, *EA*, No. 1171/3. This text supplements the discussion in Chapter II. The marginal comments (in French) of the jurist Veltwyck are reproduced in italics.

5. No one may fail, when labor pangs begin, to send for two near neighbors, under penalty.

(Impractical; many nobles and wealthy persons would not want to call in their poor neighbors.)

6. If neighbors, friends, or midwives know of some unbaptized child, they must report this within two days, under penalty.

(Unless waiting for the godparents.)

The next article deals with those who do not bear children and with traveling merchants.

7. Everyone over fourteen years old must receive the holy sacrament of the body and the blood of Christ at least once a year; this must take place between Palm Sunday and the last holiday after Easter, under. . . .

8. To be able to see who is absent, it shall be ordained that in all cities and villages the neighbors shall take mass together, reckoning as a neighborhood unit the part of the city between two bridges; villages shall be divided into four or eight parts, depending on their size.

(To these articles the mendicant monks will object, who now give communion without distinction, those who have dispensation; wherefore this could not be done without papal revocation of said privileges.)

9. If someone has traveled outside the city or village, he must, on the second or third day after his return, go to the pastor and receive the holy sacrament, thus uniting himself with all Christians in the unity of faith and the common peace. . . . He must also receive a certificate from the pastor or chaplain, after receiving the holy sacrament, to show, if necessary, to the police.

(This article is in conformity with the practice of the ancient church, but would not be practical for application.)

10. Two of the nearest neighbors shall be obliged, after receiving the holy sacrament, to inform the pastor which of their nearest neighbors is absent; of whom the pastor or a policeman appointed for the purpose shall take note and keep watch so that after his return he who was absent will not be found to be disobedient to these articles; if he is disobedient, the magistrate will be informed, and will constrain him to obey or else punish him according to imperial command.

11. No one shall contract marriage in secret; it shall take place publicly according to old ordinance and usage of the Holy Church. . . . Under penalty.

(Impracticable for those who have dispensations from their lords or bishops; contrary to custom. One cannot prove that all marriages have always been performed before the church door, though it is true that the practice of secret marriage covers many sects.)

If anyone, man or woman, unwilling to obey these orders, flees, the husband leaving his wife, or the wife leaving her husband, the remaining person shall notify the competent local officer. The remaining person shall with all diligence ascertain where the fugitive has established residence, and inform the officer, who will inform His Royal Majesty's court, where a letter shall be written to all the lords of the land, instructing them to seize the fugitive, to ban him, or otherwise to punish such persons.

(This one is not bad.)

12. Pertaining to Davidians. . . .

It shall be ordained in all cities and villages, that no one may lodge any strangers, nor rent out rooms, before first having gone to the officer of the city or village together with the prospective renter. This officer will investigate why he has come and desires to live there, and why he left the city or village of his birth. He shall not be allowed to live there, if he cannot give a certificate of good name and fame, sealed by the court of both his birthplace and the city where he last lived. The officer shall watch him carefully; this is important in order to be able to recognize the Davidians, Batenburgers, and other sects.

(For those who travel through the country otherwise than for business reasons this has been provided for by edict; for those who travel as merchants it is not practicable, unless one were to ask only for certification of their not being Anabaptist; but this would mean tolerating other heresies, by not naming the Lutherans and Oecolampadians.)

13. Against Davidians, Batenburgers, etc.

It shall be announced in every city, village, etc., that all communicants, especially men, who have come to live in a town since 1534 and who were not born there, will personally go to the place where they were born and the place where they lived before coming to their present residence, and obtain a certificate of behavior, status, name and fame, within six months.

(Not at all practicable.)

This certificate will not be issued without the testimony of three or four of his closest neighbors where he lived last, and after they have told everything they knew about him for the time he lived with them. Those close neighbors shall state this under oath. . . .

14. All letters of recommendation or certificates issued previously to departing persons shall be void and must all be renewed in due form as indicated above. This because of some Anabaptists, who by favor of friends in courts have received letters or certificates of good conduct, stating that they did not leave their city or village because of misbehavior. . . .

(Would hardly be feasible, for it would have to be announced to all the princes and cities of the East [Germany] that the Emperor considers such certificates to be invalid.)

All communicants living more than two hundred miles from their birthplace may be granted a longer time or dispensed if they are well known in the country. . . .

15. Foreigners, when they have a letter of recommendation or a certificate, will be required to take an oath, after a solemn warning, to be loyal to His Imperial Majesty and His Imperial Majesty's provinces and the city, to be obedient to all police, churches, and ordinations; and if they know or come to know anyone who does the opposite, to denounce him to the police, under penalty. No Anabaptist will take this oath.

(Impracticable for those who are on business trips. For those who come to live in this country, it is reasonable that they should swear to obey and to keep the commandments and ordinances of the country.

Van Sol thinks much of this article.)

16. None of the emigrants shall be allowed to return to the Netherlands, except with a permit sealed by the court at The Hague, Brussels, etc. No goods shall be taken out of the country, nor inheritances, but by consent of His Imperial Majesty's Secret Council. If the emigrants do not get a permit, the inheritance shall go half to the nearest blood relatives who stayed in the country, and the

other half to His Imperial Majesty's treasury. The relatives shall inform the local officers immediately of such inheritances or deaths. All the goods shall be inventoried by the officers and council members in the presence of the local heirs.

(Van Sol thinks much of this article as well, and certainly it would be desirable to prevent those who return annually to sow their errors; but the article has the weakness that Lutherans could get new permits and Anabaptists not, thus distinguishing between the sects.)

Those returning must bring a letter from the places where they have been during their stay abroad, stating how they behaved there with regard to baptism and other ordinances of the church of the land.

(This article would be very useful, if it were not for the difference and for those who travel in the country for business reasons.)

6. *The Council of Ghent asks the Regent, Maria of Hungary, to be released from the responsibility of prosecuting nineteen Mennonites handed over by the bailiff of Aalst, because there are so many other suits pending. 1551.*[9]

Madame, we recommend ourselves as very humbly as possible to your noble grace.

Madame, we have received your letters, by which you instruct us to take over the prosecution and trial of several prisoners apprehended by the bailiffs of Ghent, Saint Pierre, and Meerlebeke, fifteen in number, for certain good reasons.

Madame, said bailiff of Meerlebeke made the arrest as a representative of the grand bailiff of Aalst and in that capacity, as he has told us; in that capacity he has delivered to us not only those fifteen persons but also four more arrested on his own initiative, who had made themselves suspect by hindering him while he was bringing the others to us by virtue of the letters of Your Majesty; the result is that we now have nineteen.

Said bailiff of Meerlebeke, having been requested by the subbailiff of Ghent and the bailiff of Saint Pierre to assist in the capture, because it was outside the city, they agreed that the spot is in the territory of Aalst and thus those three officers from Ghent, Saint Pierre, and Meerlebeke made the capture within the boundaries of the Grand Bailiwick of Aalst and agreed that said prisoners should remain in the hands of the bailiff of Meerlebeke under the same conditions. Therefore, Madame, there was no disagreement nor contention for jurisdiction between those officers. Those of Ghent and Saint Pierre initiated the arrest proceedings because of certain secret warnings given them by the President of the Council.

We believe, Madame, that Your Majesty was led to assign the prosecution to us because Your Majesty supposed that there was a conflict of jurisdiction or that the officer of Meerlebeke had made the capture only in his capacity as bailiff of Meerlebeke, and should in that same capacity be willing to indict and judge said prisoners in the town of Meerlebeke, which, however, would not be a convenient place for such a trial.

Therefore, Madame, though said prisoners have been delivered to us, we have not begun proceedings against them, hoping that Your Majesty would no longer esteem, after being thus informed, that the prosecution and trial belong to us; hoping that Your Majesty will not charge us with such a great hindrance to our normal judicial procedure, considering the multitude of trials with which

9 June 3, 1551. Ghent State, *RVBW*, reg. 20, fol. 128 ff. (French original).

we are charged, and that the eight Anabaptists whom we arrested three months ago have caused us a great delay, and if we should have to begin with the indictment of that large number of nineteen the delay would be greatly increased. As a result current cases could not be dealt with for a long time, to the great disadvantage of many poor plaintiffs and even at present we have an ecclesiastical suit for maintenance pending, which if it is not decided before next Saint John's Day will mean the loss of the revenues of an entire year.

Speaking with all reverence and subject to Your noble correction, the indictment in this case belongs not only by right but also according to the exact text of His Imperial Majesty's edict, to the subaltern and inferior judges, who in this case are obviously those of Aalst, a notable assembly of good repute, administering justice in the city of Aalst, as well as the Lord of Courriere, his lieutenant, and the bailiff of Meerlebeke. They agreed and do agree, and would have taken said prisoners to Aalst the same day, with no objection from any other magistrates, had it not been for the letter Your Majesty had sent them. Wherefore, Madame, it seemed to us that we should inform Your Majesty and beseech You, as we do by the present letter, very humbly, not to take away from those of Aalst the prosecution and trial which belong to them, and not to charge us with anything which is not of our competence, and to avoid delay in our ordinary justice that it may please Your Majesty, for reasons stated above, to leave said prosecution to those of Aalst.

In so doing, Your Majesty will make great advancement to the ordinary justice of this Council and also follow the terms of the afore-mentioned edicts.

Madame, we pray God. . . .

7. *The Council of Flanders urges all city authorities to support the Inquisition. 1551.*[10]

The members of the Council. . . .

Dearly beloved, because it has been commanded and ordained unto us and unto all other officers and vassals of His Imperial Majesty, our fearsome Lord, to give all assistance, help, and support to execute and accomplish the charge and commission of the Inquisitor of Heresy and his assessors and adjuncts, so it falls to us to order, charge, and command you, in the name of the Emperor, our fearsome Lord, and by his commission, that you and all of your men are particularly urged by said inquisitor, assessors, adjuncts, and anyone of their party, to give them help, support, and assistance to summon persons, to use force in case of arrest and detention, doing this with such a sense of duty and diligence that there will be no reason for them to complain that they are hindered by lack of support.

Dearly beloved, God be with you.

8. *Account of the execution of Margriete van den Berghe, Jooris Cooman, Naentkin Bornaige, and Wouter van der Weyden. 1515.*[11]

In consequence of the great and vigorous persecution of true Christians in every part of the Netherlands, four pious Christians, among others, fled in 1551

---

10 July 4, 1551. Ghent State, *RVBW*, reg. 20, fol. 39. The Council had received instructions on this subject from the emperor on April 18; Ghent State, *Series 93*, reg. 9, fol. 235voff.

11 Van Braght, *Mirror*, II, p. 106. The execution took place on April 11; van Braght gives only the year.

from Lier in Brabant to Ghent in Flanders. Their names were Jooris, Wouter, Grietgen, and Naentgen. They had not long resided there before they were betrayed by a Judas and taken from their homes to the Gravensteen.[12] There they cheerfully thanked God and sang His praise that they were counted worthy to suffer for His name. When assailed by the monks and other sophists, they freely confessed their faith, from which no deceitful subtlety could turn them. They valiantly withstood with the truth the seducers who sought to destroy their souls, and were condemned to death by virtue of the Imperial mandate for falling away from the Roman Church, despising infant baptism, and being baptized upon confession of faith. They were sentenced to be burned at the stake without being strangled. They thanked the court, and Grietgen said, "My Lords, three stakes can be spared, we can all four die at one; for we are all spiritually of one mind." They were glad in the Lord, greatly praising Him. Naentgen said, "This is the day for which I have earnestly longed."

Eight monks then came to torment them, but they would not receive their counsels. Grietgen said, "Take off your long robes and teach yourselves before you undertake to teach others." As sheep to the slaughter they were led to death. The monks accompanied them, to whom they said, "Stay back, leave us in peace, for we know you well and do not wish to hear you." Having ascended the scaffold, Jooris said to the people, "Be it known to you that we do not die for theft, murder, or heresy." At this the monks were enraged, and contradicted it. They then fell on their knees, prayed to God, and arose and kissed one another with the kiss of peace. As they with glad countenances addressed the people, the monks, to hinder them, went and stood before them; but one of the people called out, "Stand back, you raging antichrists, and let them speak!"

Wouter said, "Citizens of Ghent, we do not suffer as heretics, nor as Lutherans, who hold in one hand a beer mug and in the other a Testament, dishonoring the Word of God and walking in drunkenness. We die for the pure truth!" Then the executioner hanged each of them by a noose to the stake, but did not strangle them. They strengthened one another, saying, "Let us fight valiantly, for this is our last suffering; henceforth we shall rejoice with God in endless joy." While hanging in pain, before the fire was kindled, Jooris fell through the noose, and Wouter cried, "Oh, brother, be of good courage!" "O Lord!" exclaimed Jooris, "in Thee do I trust, strengthen my faith!" The fire then began to burn. They cried out, "O God our Father, into Thy hands we commend our spirits." Thus they offered up their sacrifice according to the will of the Lord, and their faith was tried like gold in the fire, and found good and accepted by God.

9. A view of the witnessing methods of the brotherhood. May, 1557.[13]

Philip, by the grace of God King of Castille, Leon, Aragon, England. . . . Be it known to everyone present and future, that we have received the humble supplication of Roelandt van Loo, son of Roelandt Vlesschouwere, seller of fish, burgher and resident of Ghent, certifying that Roelandt is an honest, peaceable man, descended from good honest parents, who taught and directed Roelandt to live according to the old order of the common and Catholic Church, which Roelandt has always tried to follow.

---

12 Literally "Count's Castle." This building evidently was used as prison and courtroom.

13 Ghent City, *Series 93*, reg. T, fol. 417vof. Where the document refers to Roelandt as "suppliant" the translation inserts his name.

However, last summer there came to him one evening Victor Seysins, who also is a butcher, and asked Roelandt to go for a walk with him, to which Roelandt agreed, suspecting nothing.

Victor led Roelandt to the Burchstede, where he asked him to wait a moment on the street; Roelandt waited. Victor left, went into a side street, and shortly returned with a young man, absolutely unknown to Roelandt, who had never seen him before. This young man invited him to go along for a walk outside the gates early in the morning, saying, "You will hear something there which will please you very much."

For this reason Roelandt went, on the day fixed by the same person, and waited for a moment at the agreed place, where the said unknown person also arrived. Roelandt was led to a grain field, without knowing where he was going; the same person only said, "Follow me." When they reached the grain field, Roelandt saw sitting in it about ten or twelve people and three or four girls or women, who were all unknown to Roelandt, since he had never had any dealings with them before.

There Roelandt also heard another young man, unknown, speak for a long time, and he remembers among other things, "that everyone should beware of evil and improve his life and that all drunkards and adulterers would not enter the kingdom of God." Afterward one of the girls or women had black cherries in her lap, which were shared by all; then the group broke up and everyone went home.

A certain time after this meeting the same Victor Seysins again came to Roelandt and asked him again to go walking, which he did. Victor brought him past the Cuup Gate which stands in said city and into an alley, where Victor knocked on the door of a house with which Roelandt was not acquainted, which he had never seen. Opening the door Victor entered, telling Roelandt to come along, which he did. Entering the house, he met three or four people, all of them unknown to him, as he had never seen them before, one of whom stated publicly "that God is to be greatly praised and thanked, for all things were now revealed which had been hidden so long." They had several talks and discussions, which Roelandt does not remember, because he did not understand.

Another time there came to Roelandt by a similar ruse one Jacob, a weaver by trade, one of those whom Roelandt had seen in the grain field, as he told him, and brought Roelandt into a house near the presbytery, where an indigo dyer lived, where ten or twelve people were present: Victor Seysins, Willem Villeers, and Gheert de Cortewaghencruudere, but Roelandt did not know all of them. A stranger, also unknown to Roelandt, was preaching, but Roelandt does not remember what he said. Another time it was in the same house, early in the morning, some time after the first meeting. About seven or eight people were present, including Jacob the Weaver. A fat man without a beard was speaking.

Roelandt did not desire to attend more such meetings nor listen to these people, therefore he avoided them for a long time and was on his guard. Several times people came to see him in the shop and on the street and asked why he no longer desired their society. He answered that he did not care for it and was busy with other things; finally the same fat man came and asked him the same questions, which Roelandt answered, saying he was too busy. The fat man asked him where he lived and whether he would consent to let four or five people meet in the evening in his home. Roelandt allowed this, without knowing who the people were whom they would bring to his house.

So the same man came to Roelandt's house, bringing eight or nine people along: Laureyns de Brauwere, Pieter de Cleerck, a miller, Willem Villeers, Gheert de Cortewaghencruudere, and some others not known to Roelandt. The same fat man preached from the Old and New Testaments without ever mentioning rebaptism; they left his house again. This was about three or four months ago and afterward Roelandt never met the same people again and never attended their meetings and he never had any evil feelings, even during those meetings and evil unseemly sermons, toward our Mother, the Holy Church, and he went to confession and received the sacraments and other things, as a child of the Holy Church should and must do, until Easter 1556, when he was in Holland on a business trip. He had also abstained for some time, because of those preachers who were attacking it, although he never agreed with their attacks.[14]

10. Proceedings against Mennonites of Bruges arrested June 24 and 29, 1558.[15]

Done at the Steen, June 24. Present: the Burgomaster of the Council, the Burgomaster of the guilds, the Governor, and Jan van Heede, Council member.

Lievekin van der Veste, son of Jan Verveste, twelve years old, ribbon weaver, says that he was born at Ghent and lived there at the Techelrie for ten or eleven years; then he left for Holland with his father and mother, to Amsterdam for about a year; from there they came to Bruges and lived there for about two or three months.

Says he was christened in the St. Jans Church at Ghent and that he went to church; always went to confession with his father and mother till about three or four years ago and not any more only because his father and mother will not allow it. Says that they came back from Holland because there was no work for his father; his father now works here for Franchois Dhondt. Says he hears his father and mother say, "Things are better now than before."

He saw his father and mother meet with several people, up to seven or eight, at his home, but does not know what they said, because they sent him out to play. His brothers and sisters are Hanskin, Betkin, Cyncken, Michielkin. The latter two live at Ghent, Cyncken with the man in the house " 't mortaens hooft" across the street from the Franciscan Friars, together with her uncle, with whom she has lived ever since she was two, and Michielkin with Jacop Vroyelick, on the other side of the Jacobin Bridge. Cyncken is seven years old and Michielkin about eight. Besides these his father had three other children; Cornelis, who died when he was three, Neelken when she was two, and Zusannekin when she was one year old. None of them were baptized in the church or in a basin at home or anywhere else, since, as Lievekin heard his father say, "they know better now." He has not been to church for four or five years, but he has prayed at every meal at home and sometimes reads the Lord's Prayer but did not learn the Hail Mary because his mother told him that this was not good.[16]

The two persons who were taken captive with him were his cousins, who live

---

14 There follows the declaration of Roelandt's acquittal.

15 Bruges City, *Bouc van den Steene,* 1558-59, fol. 89-95.

16 Marginal note: "On August 16, 1558, the inquisitor of heresy, Titelmanns, released from prison Lievekin and Betkin Verveste, under condition that they promised to go to mass and to confession before Master Jan van der Haghe, Th.B., and that they should be sent to Neelkin van Deinze, sister of Vincken Verwee, mother of the children, as it has been ordained by Milords the magistrates and the Council" (fol. 89vo).

at Nieuport. One is a miller named Jacob, the other a cabinetmaker named Hanskin; he had heard them say at the table on the evening they were taken prisoner that they thanked God that they had found the truth and it grieved them that they had erred so long.

Betkin van der Veste, sister of Lievekin, thirteen years old, says that she was born at Ghent and lived there with Miss van der Catulle for about six months. Her father came from Holland to get her from there half a year ago, and she again lived with her father and his family at Amsterdam, until they came to Bruges. Previously she had lived at Antwerp with a Gheraewert Harinck to learn sewing and lived with him till the city officers came to look for him because he read the Bible, but they didn't find him, and she doesn't know whether he has been caught since then. Says it was about four or five years ago that she heard her father and mother say that they know better now, and that the baptism practiced here is not right, but they understood now that there is another baptism; people should be baptized when they understand and change their lives, when they no longer lie and deceive.

She says further that it is about half a year since her father and mother were rebaptized. The baptism was performed off the Teghelrie near the Oof Bridge, where Willem van Leuvene lived, who was the leader, and several persons were present, of whom some have been burned at Ghent, to wit, said Willem and Vincken his wife.

Says that she does not go to church and never went during the time she lived with her father and mother, which is about six months; at Amsterdam her father left her with a sick woman, whom she attended until about a month before they came to Bruges. At Ghent, living with Miss van der Catulle, she went to confession to Friar Pieter de Backere, a Jacobin monk, who punished her because she believed more what her father said than what Friar Pieter said.

On the day she was arrested, her father and mother had come out to see Hanskin, her cousin, and Jacob the miller, living near Nieuport. Hanskin, her cousin, lives there.[17]

Hanskin van der Veste, brother of the above, fifteen years old, says that it is about five years that his father and mother knew of the new sect and that his friends therefore took him away from them and brought him to the home of Michiel de Draettreckere, who, however, also read the Bible, and then after about a year to the home of Jan de Meij, who is a shingler, whom he left about June 13, 1557. From then on he lived with his father at Amsterdam and Bruges; during which time he went neither to confession nor to church, because he had heard that that was not right, in such a way that he halfway believed it; but concerning baptism or rebaptism he knows nothing, except that a certain Willem van Leuvene used to come to the home of his father and mother, but they did not tell him what they did.

Says that he has been working for about a month at Oudenburch with Valentyn, a shingler; furthermore that his father and mother had had to leave Ghent because of the Scriptures and he understood that they were Anabaptists and that they were grieved by the fact that Hanskin did not join them and accept their

---

17 Marginal note: "Said Hanskin, who on July 28 escaped from Het Steen [the prison], having filed a great iron grate with two broken knives, is mentioned in the *Informatiebouk*, fol. 70."

teachings; furthermore that he heard them say that they baptized no one unless they desired it.

Vincken Verwee, wife of Jan Verveste, born at Deinse, says that she has lived at Ghent ever since she was eleven years old and about five years ago she accepted another faith, leaving the Roman Church, mass, and the other sacraments, because they are founded on human inventions and idolatries, giving as a reason: "The vineyard which my father did not plant. . . ."[18] Later she was rebaptized, about three years ago, in the city of Ghent at the home of a person she does not know, on Holstraet. He was Gillis van Haecke, she remembers, who was beheaded at Antwerp.[19] She says she would not like to die as he died, for he gave up his faith. Says she finds nothing of God in the church and that she has not had her last child baptized. She also did not have her older and living children rebaptized because they had not asked for it and were not mature enough yet; should her youngest child die without baptism, she would not have it baptized before death. . . .

Her husband had been baptized together with her the same day and hour in the same house. She came in contact with this faith for the first time because her husband had to do with rhetoric and in this connection had to do with the Scriptures and she listened carefully and finally they joined this sect, to which also belonged Hans van den Broucke, her cousin, and Jacob, also arrested, both of them rebaptized, but she does not know exactly when; they call each other brethren and sisters.

This Vincken has been visited by the two sworn municipal midwives, because she had said she was ill; these declared under oath that they had not found her to be nearing childbirth. September 11, at about noon she gave birth to a male child. The midwives said that the child had not yet begun to live; it was taken to a foster mother the same day.[20] September 16 the jailer reported that Vincken had a swollen head and a surgeon should be sent; the report was made to the Council which decided that the expenses should be charged to the inquisitor whose prisoner she was. Vincken died in the prison from the swelling which descended from her head and suffocated her September 20. She was buried at night, with the authorization of the secretary in the inquisitor's absence, at St. Jans in unconsecrated earth, because of her impenitence and obstinacy.[21]

Jan Verveste says he was rebaptized at Ghent on Holstraet about five years ago. He does not know, however, the exact time he left the Roman Church and stopped attending mass. Says his living children have not been rebaptized because they are not yet wise enough. His last child, which died before it was one year old, was not baptized; he believes that Hanskin and Jacob, both in prison, have been rebaptized, but does not know where or when.

18 Matt. 15:13. The term "vineyard" instead of "planting" does not appear in any known Dutch New Testament; it was probably inserted because of an association of the imagery of Matt. 15 with that of John 15.

19 Hacke, i.e., Aachen; cf. the mention of the apostate Gillis van Aken above.

20 The statement of the midwives cannot mean that the child was stillborn or died at birth, for it was taken to a foster mother to be cared for. The midwives are probably denying that the embryo was alive at the time of their examination; contemporary canon law dated the inception of life anywhere from the fortieth to the 116th day after conception.

21 Translator's note: The above paragraphs are presumably marginal glosses or later insertions in the archival source, though not labeled as such, since their report about Vincken's illness and death here precedes a later report of further interrogations of the Verveste family.

Says that he still intends to remain firm in his faith till the end, and still does not believe in the Roman Church, the mass, the sacraments, and all the things they do in that church.[22]

Hans van den Broucke, unmarried, linen weaver, born at Ghent, says that about two years ago he was rebaptized in that city at the home of a shoemaker not far from the house of Lieven de Ooghe, out of obedience to the Scriptures, for he only knows about one baptism in the Scriptures and that is the one received by those who have come to the age of discretion; he received it at the age of twenty or twenty-one. He is not doubtful about it, for he is consoled by the Scriptures; furthermore he does not follow the Roman Church or the seven sacraments, which are not based on the Scriptures, but are human inventions.

He, Hans, lives at Oostende near the quai at the East Mill, with the miller, Jacob de Zwarte. He has discussed the Scriptures with him but does not remember telling him that he had been rebaptized; says he does not want to accuse or betray him; says that he has a father, living at Ghent at the place called "up de mude," who is a carpenter, named Jan van den Broucke, with whom he discussed the Scriptures but he did not want to believe him.

Decided by the Council that if this Jan van den Broucke does not confess, he shall be strangled at the stake and burned to powder; if he confesses, he shall be executed with the sword. Decided October 13, 1558. Said Hans was executed by fire October 15.

Coppen de Zwarte, born at Nijpkerke near Belle, married, says that he lived at Oostende recently and before that at Onscote; he first became acquainted with Hans van den Broucke, the prisoner, within the last half year or thereabouts, during which time he spoke with him about the Scriptures. Says that he has nothing for the Roman Church, nor the other sacraments and her ceremonies; no more for the sacrament of the altar than for that of marriage and others. He was rebaptized less than a year ago. He has a child, three or four months old, which has not been baptized in the church although his wife would have preferred it. Says further, when asked when and by whom he was baptized, that he does not have to answer, that this is the way witches ask questions; he went to school, learned to understand God's Word, and believed. He confesses that he received the formality of baptism in the city of Onscote, in a house on Noordstrate formerly belonging to Jan de Teldere and occupied by Jasper Sceemaeckere, formerly a master, now working for someone else. Does not know who baptized him, but has discussed the Scripture with Hans van den Broucke, Jan Verveste and his wife, and one Lieven van Male, from Ghent, who died in Zeeland. He had no other teacher but God the Lord. He has a father in Onscote, named Jan de Zwarte, living on Noordstrate, a miller; says that he argued with him about the Scriptures and he answered that he hoped he was doing the right.

Decided by the Council on October 6 to hang Coppen on a pulley over the hearth and examine him, using a whip.

Done October 7, nothing confessed.

---

22 Marginal note (chronologically out of place): "This Jan died in the castle and was buried, with authorization of the secretary in the absence of the inquisitor, in the dump at St. Jan's, because of his recalcitrance. He died August 24th about ten o'clock in the evening, having been visited by Master Franchois Capart, the sworn surgeon of the city, and was buried the next day, August 25, at noon (fol. 91)."

Decided by the Council to execute Jacob or Coppen de Zwarte like Hans van den Broucke. Ordered August 13. Executed by fire August 15.

Done at the Steen, June 29, 1558. Present: the magistrate, the Burgomaster of the guilds, Sayon, two Council members.

Livine, wife of Jan Verveste, questioned again about her accomplices, says that she knew and knows Jan Verpoorte, tailor, at Ghent, but does not know where he lives; she knows that he belongs to their sect. Also Jan, called Squinting Jan, also at Ghent, but she has not seen him nor spoken with him since she fled from Ghent. Jan Pierson, silk weaver, she neither knows nor has heard about. She has heard about Jan van den Driessche, but does not know him nor where he lives; she has heard that he lives at Danzig and belongs to her sect. She knew Pieter Bonne, brewer, about three years ago. He lived at Ghent near the New Bridge and was arrested at his house because he refused to take an oath, which they are not allowed to do. She thinks he probably weakened, for he was released from prison. Jooris Wippe, weaver, imprisoned at Dort; she knows him and has been in his home at Dort, but does not know where his wife is. Nor does she know Hendrick, the miller from Oostende. She declares that she holds to her sect and all the points stated in her first confession. She has been married to Jan Verveste eighteen or nineteen years.

Jan Verveste, questioned again, says that he knows Jan Verpoorte, the tailor, and that he belonged to his sect, but he has not seen him nor spoken with him since he left Ghent. Does not know where he is. Jan, named Squinting Jan, he knew in Ghent, but has never seen him since then. He came to live at Bruges at about the beginning of Lent and has been working for Franchois Dhondt. Knows no one else who might be of his sect, neither Jan van den Driessche nor Jooris Wippe nor Hendrick the miller. He has heard of and once ate with Pieter Bonne; he holds to his belief and his first confession.

Hans van den Broucke, questioned again, says that Hendrick the miller, living at Oostende in the East Mill, is his master, but that he does not belong to his sect, being a drunkard like the others; except that he once told Hans that he believed that it was good and right, but that he could come no closer. Says that about a month ago he was at the home of Jan Verveste for three or four days, discussing the Scriptures. Questioned about his accomplices or fellow apostles, says that according to God's Word he should accuse no one, and therefore names no one, refusing to do so. Asked specifically about Jan Verpoorte, he says he knew him at Ghent and saw and spoke with him at Bruges, about two years ago, but does not know where he lives, for they do not ask each other where they live, because that is vanity. He knew Squinting Jan and spoke with him at Ghent about three years ago; does not think he is one of theirs and does not know where he is. Does not know Joos Pierson or Pieter Bonne, except that he saw him once.

. . .[23] Against him nor against his wife; concerning Jooris Wippe, says that he has worked at his house, but he was not Scripture-minded then.

Jacob de Zwarte, questioned again, says he was at the home of Jan Verveste once more just before Pentecost; says that he has discussed the Scriptures with his wife and with Tannekin, his sister-in-law, but they answered that they could not grasp it. Asked about Jan Verpoorte and Squinting Jan, says he does not know them; he does know divers persons of the world, who are not of the true

---

23 A part of fol. 93 is damaged.

faith; does not know Pieter Bonne or Jooris Wippe, holds to his first confession. Says he was never formally married to his wife, but that they promised each other to stay together till death; they prefer this promise to marriage in the church or according to the ceremonies of the church.

Betkin Verveste, questioned again, says that she knows no one associated with her father but Hanskin van den Broucke and Jacob de Zwarte, who have been at her father's home once more.

Hanskin and Lievekin, further questioned: Hanskin: They know no accomplices and know not what is right or wrong except that they heard their father say that there were evil teachers in the church. Lievekin says they know Hans van den Broucke and Jacob de Zwarte, but no others.

On July 29 Lievekin and Betkin Verveste described how their brother Hanskin, who was imprisoned with them in the same room, broke out, assisted by Cornelis Jansins, a peddler, who was also imprisoned in the same room, and that they escaped in this way on July 28. . . .[23] With two knives with teeth Cornelis and Hanskin sawed off two iron bars from a large iron grate; those bars were thick, one and one-half inches square, that means eight inches around, and Hanskin and Cornelis began to file and saw at about eight in the morning and continued when there was opportunity, and filled the cuts with wax. None of the knives had had teeth but Cornelis and Hanskin had cut and filed them that way. When they were almost through they used a square stick to force the bars off; then tore their sheets in strips, as well as Lievekin's, knotting the pieces together, fastening one end at the drain before they jumped out and let themselves down at about eleven o'clock in the evening. Lievekin and Betkin also say that Cornelis had previously signaled to his wife from the window with straws to bring ropes, but she had not understood.

Excerpts of the answers of Jan van der Veste, arrested on a charge of heresy.[24] Says he was at a meeting here in Bruges at the house of a certain Jacob, living between the St. Cathelina Gate and the Ghent Gate in a large house.[25] Martin den Twijndere of Ghent, whose wife is Neelken, did the exhorting. Martin and Neelken are rebaptized; there were several people whom he does not know and his own wife was there as well. Another time he was at a meeting where the same Martin preached, across the street from Jan de Mutsescherdere, who used to live in Ghent, Anabaptist, in whose home Jan van der Veste lived and went to the same meetings. Jan de Mutsescherdere has a wife Tannekin who is not an Anabaptist. Jacob and his wife were also present, he believes.

Says also that the wife of Martin den Twijndere was at the meeting at the Mutsescherdere's near the potter; that Martin lived here near the St. Cathelina Gate around the time that he, Jan Verveste, was arrested in an alley near the pottery by the High Bridge. Jan Mutsescherdere, living near St. Claire, was also at the meeting at the home of Jacob near the High Bridge. When there was a meeting this Jacob came to get him.

24 This was apparently originally a separate text. Since it refers to a repeated refusal of Jan Verveste and Jacob de Zwarte to reveal information about their teachers, it is later than the main body of the above texts, immediately prior to the inserted reports on their torture and death.

25 Marginal note (partly damaged): "Decided . . . to investigate the houses where the meetings are usually held, situated . . . then haul the persons out of those houses and arrest them. Decided August 23, 1558."

9

Says also on further questioning that the house where the meetings were held between the St. Cathelina Gate and the Ghent Gate has a fence in front with a large gate and borders on the moat, which was convenient because they keep cows. The first meeting was held last Easter, early in the morning, so that the sermon was given during sunrise. About fifteen or sixteen persons were present, among them Hans van den Broucke and Franchois, who he thinks is a widower, who once carried the announcement when a meeting was to be held. Further questioned, says that the Jacob's house, where the meetings were held near the St. Cathelina Gate, is opposite the house of Jan de Bonnetscherdere, where he, Jan Verveste, lodged.[26] He never noticed whether Jacob has a trade. Asked how many meetings he had attended at Bruges, he answers three or four, in three different homes: at Jacob's near the pottery; at the home of Martin den Twijndere, who lived at the High Bridge near the potter, where Martin himself preached; after he had finished there had been a certain Franche, born at Ypres, single, a woolen weaver, who also explained God's Word, but Martin was much better than Franche. . . .[27] Lived in that house and tell when this meeting was held, saying that he hoped never to tell it.

Jacob de Zwarte, questioned again, says he attended no meetings in Bruges or Oostende, nor in Onscote; he had done his duty to try to bring his wife and Tannekin, his sister-in-law, to his convictions and doctrines, but so far he could not convince them, so that they were far from being ready for baptism. His father-in-law as well does not share his views, and never has since he has known him; questioned about his teachers or accomplices, says he will not name any of them.

February 16, 1558 [1559], there appeared before the Council of Bruges Jacop Raes and the substitute of the magistrate, reporting that the goods left by Jan Verveste and Vincken, his wife, both Anabaptists imprisoned in Het Steen, have not yet been confiscated and booked under extraordinary receipts, as he was formerly instructed to do. He requests authorization to inventory and sell as representative of the interests of . . . this city, the above-named goods, to which Milord the magistrate consented. Accordingly it was also ordered by the Council that justice be done and immediately gave to Raes the substitute of Milord the magistrate, the keys of the house of Jan and Vincken Verveste. Done February 16, 1558 [1559].

11. The inquisitor Titelman sentences five Mennonites at Ghent.[28]

Copy of the sentence pronounced by the inquisitor of the Christian faith against five persons, heretics, named below, and turned over to the Council as to the secular justice on February 17, 1559 [1560].

In the case of inquisition tried before us, Pieter Titelman, Th.L., Dean of the collegial church of St. Hermes at Ronse, delegated as inquisitor of our holy Christian faith in Flanders, between Master Claes de Hondt, executive of aforesaid office of the inquisition, functioning ex officio as prosecutor, on the one hand, and you:

26 Jan de Bonnetscherdere is identical with the Jan de Mutsescherdere referred to earlier.
27 Several lines of text are seriously damaged.
28 Ghent City, *Crime*, 1555-61, fol. 193 ff.

Joos de Vynck, son of Jacob van Poperinge, about twenty-seven; Joos de Vlaminck, son of Gillis van Brugghe, about twenty-nine; Michiel van Houcke, son of Pieters van Nevele, about twenty-three; Joos van den Walle, son of Andries van Ghendt, about thirty-two; and Sanders van Grimberghe, son of Gillis, about thirty-one years old, as defendants on the other hand.

Considering the articles and the accusation of the prosecutor and your answers to these accusations and interrogations, as defendants, together with all those things which you subsequently desired to say, answer, and allege in order to explain that your conduct has been right, we find that you . . . ,[29] all and severally, simple laymen and artisans, have been misbehaving for a long time, have listened to some persons and books, believed them, followed them, and have discussed the Holy Scriptures with them in secret meetings and tried to understand, according to your own opinion, contrary to the universal and manifest faith, sacraments, and teachings of our Mother, the Holy Roman Apostolic and Universal Christian Church, which has been publicly taught, preached, and daily practiced everywhere in this country, where you were born, baptized, and raised, as well as in other Christian countries from olden times, as you know very well, according to your own statements.

Since in contradiction with that faith and Holy Church, you have accepted and held many evil, false, scandalous, heretical, and schismatic opinions, reproved and condemned by Holy Scriptures as well as by the several Ecumenical Councils and statements of the holy fathers, also stubbornly persisting in them, among others:

That infant baptism as practiced in the Holy Roman Church is useless and worthless;

That one should be baptized only after having believed and understood;

That baptism, even if received consciously, does not bring salvation, but is only a sign of obedience and a good conscience;

That the children who die without baptism are nonetheless saved;

That Christ Jesus is not truly present in flesh and blood in the sacrament of the altar;

That the same sacrament is an idol and that it is idolatry to worship it;

That the sacrifice of the mass is a human institution and that it is idolatry to hear mass;

That one is not obliged to confess his sins to the priest in order to receive forgiveness, and that the priest does not have the power to hear sinners' confessions and to absolve them;

That it is wrong to call upon Mary, the Mother of Christ, or other saints of God, asking them to pray to God on our behalf;

That there is no purgatory for the souls after this life and that it is useless to perform the sacrifice of the mass, prayer, or alms on behalf of the dead;

That the souls of the dead, yea even those of the blessed Mother and Virgin Mary and the apostles, are not yet in heaven and will not be there until the Last Judgment;

That it is not permitted to swear or take an oath, even if one is asked to do so by the court to give a true testimony;

29 The names of the accused are repeated here in the original.

That all days are equal, thus one is not obliged to celebrate Sundays or holy
days, and also one need not eat different foods on Fridays, Saturdays, or Lent
than on other days;

That we need not do or believe anything but what is expressly taught or commanded by the Holy Scriptures;

That the Roman Church is not the true Christian Church, but that idolatry is
practiced in this church;

That the pope of Rome is the Antichrist;

That Christ did not descend into hell;

That Christ Jesus did not receive His human nature from the substance of His
Blessed Mother, the Virgin Mary;

That there is only one person in the Holy Trinity, that is, Christ Jesus.

As a result of these your opinions, errors, and heresies, together with others
involved in this case, you, Joos de Vynck, Joos de Vlaminck, Michiel van Houcke,
and Joos van den Walle, have actually had yourselves rebaptized some years ago,
forsaking and despising your infant baptism, and you, Sanders van Grimberghe,
were and still are, according to your statements, desirous to be baptized, forsaking
and despising your infant baptism. And all of you have, years ago, ceased to go
to church, mass, confession, and the holy sacrament of the altar, despising the
same, about which opinions, errors, and heresies we have at several times zealously
warned and taught with several passages from the Holy Scriptures and have
prayed that you might return to the true faith of our Mother, the Holy Roman
Apostolic Christian Church, to be accepted as a child which has erred and asked
for mercy, into the lap of its mother. We gave you to that end several opportuni-
ties, but in spite of all this you have always stubbornly and obstinately remained
in your heresies and still speak scandalously and blasphemously about the Holy
Church, her teachings and her sacraments; so that you give us no reason to hope
for amendment.

Thus having carefully weighed and considered all these things together with
other facts and the merits of your case and having discussed those things which
pertain to the law with several learned, discreet, and pious men of divinity and
law; having considered as well the teachings of the worthy Apostle Saint Paul,
the elected vessel of Christ, who says that a heretic who has been admonished
once and again and still does not repent is condemned by his own judgment;
invoking the name of Christ, in the presence of the Holy Gospel, with God
Almighty and His righteousness before our eyes, sitting to do right and administer
justice, we say, show, declare, and pronounce by this our definitive written judgment, that you . . .29 have been and still are obstinate and stiff-necked heretics
and schismatics; that each of you has been and still is since the time when you
committed the offense under the papal ban, excommunicated and cut off from
the fellowship of the Holy Church as stubborn and impenitent.

Thus we expel you all and severally, really and in fact, from the fold and
the spiritual jurisdiction of said Christian Church and leave you to the secular
arm, but not without praying by the mercy of God that they will moderate your
sentence without danger of death; the expenses of this inquisition and trial,
which we bestow on our prosecutor or other deputies, shall be paid out of your
respective goods, regardless of who is competent to confiscate them.

Thus done and pronounced by the mouth of Master Pieter Titelman, Inquisitor, judging in the city hall of the city of Ghent, in the tribunal with Friar Pieter

de Backere, prior of the Dominicans at Ghent, Inquisitor of his Order, on February 17, 1559 [1560]; present: Pieter van Overbeke, bailiff; Jooris Vyts and Lieven van Heurne, Council members; Friar Franchois Rufelaert and Jan Pyn and a large crowd of people, both secular and clergy, and my notary.[30]

12. *Jacques de Rore and Herman Vlecwijk appear before the authorities, April-June, 1569.*[31]

Examination at the Castle of Bruges on April 22, 1569, by the Lord Mayors Dixmude, Clercq, and Masin.

Jacques de Rore, about thirty-seven years old, born at Courtrai, weaver by trade, living at Meenen, which he left about two months ago, has since then been selling felt hats which his son bought at Bruges.

Says he was arrested at Nieuwerhaven, while coming from Nijmegen, together with Herman, born in the country of Cleve; as they met the officer he had passed them by, but he returned immediately and spoke to said Herman, saying that he belonged to the new religion, but Jacques did not know what he meant. And because Jacques was there too, the officer assumed that he was of the same religion and arrested both of them.

Says he does not remember having discussed the Scriptures. Asked when he went to confession for the last time, he says at Courtrai and doesn't know how long ago; thinks about eighteen years ago; has forgotten the name of his confessor. He had ceased to confess because he did not think it right before God and because he understood that the confessor was supposed to be allowed to forgive sins, which he cannot believe; only God can do that.

In the same way he did not go to the holy sacrament, because he does not believe that God Almighty is present in the sacrament in flesh and blood as they claim. Says he does not follow any persons, but follows God's Word.

Says he has no knowledge of Latin and that wisdom does not depend on Latin. Says he has been instructed thus by persons who think like Menno and since he cannot find anything better he will stand by it until someone comes along who can show him something better.

He has also instructed other persons in several places in Courtrai, in Meenen, in and outside the city of Bruges; he cannot tell the exact time. Further says he cannot tell the names of the places, to avoid accusing anyone. He was freed about two years ago. Has been living in Bruges for about two years in the house of Simon de la Ville in Oudenburch.

At the same time:

Herman Vlecwijk, born at Kervendonck in the country of Cleve, about thirty-five years of age, tailor by trade, has traveled much in many countries and set up shop at Bruges on the Oudenburch about four years ago. Afterward he lived in " 't bosken" on Steen Street; he moved away because they were seeking to arrest

---

30 Marginal note (fol. 193vo): "On March 1, 1559 [1560], the gentlemen Jan Heyman and Michiel Dhooghe, members of Council, Master Jan de Bois, pensionary, and Roelandt van Hembyze, secretary, were sent by the Council to the accused to examine whether they persisted in the errors, opinions, and misunderstandings declared in the sentence, offering them various explanations and persuasions to bring them back to the true Christian faith. However, they persisted in their above-mentioned errors and misconceptions."

31 Bruges State, *Crime*, 1569-73, fols. 7vof., 9vo, 14 voff., 18voff., 21, 22vo.

him because they said he was Scripture-minded;[32] but how can he be Scripture-minded when he can neither read nor write?

It has been about four years, he thinks, that he has not gone to confession. His last confessor was the Dean of Kersterhede, a tall man. He ceased to confess because he thought it was not right. Has been outside to the sermons and knew some people who were executed by fire about five years ago in Bruges; one was named Adriaen, whose surname he does not know. This Adriaen was the first one to instruct him.

Met Jacques, examined here, at Nijmegen on a boat and had made clothing for him earlier in Bruges, but Herman had never been in his home. Was arrested between Schoudere and Nieuwerhaven. Was baptized about four years ago at Ghent. Was imprisoned once before together with above-named Adriaen and others in the Castle of Bruges. Knows who baptized him, but does not desire to name him. He had never met him before he was baptized and he lives in or near the country of Cleve. His name is Jan; his surname he does not know.

He came to Bruges to collect and to pay some debts.

Was imprisoned in Bruges for about five weeks and was released without punishment. He sent his wife and children to Cologne, in the country of Cleve.

In the Chamber, April 27, 1569.

Jacques de Rore, born at Courtrai, living at Meenen, is married and left his wife at Meenen; has since asked her to come but does not know whether she is coming. Says he was never imprisoned before; insists under examination that those who instructed him first, living at Courtrai, are dead. Laurens van Gelder was executed at Antwerp by the Margrave of Antwerp and Simoen van Leerberghe is dead.

Confesses having been present when some people were baptized near Courtrai, probably in the parish of Marck, in a wood; the baptizer was called Gillis van Aken, who was executed at Antwerp, but had recanted.

Jacques was baptized in the same wood and four others with him; three of them died a natural death. The fourth is Jooris Simoensz, but because of the Inquisition he could not stay in Courtrai, and thus he had not seen him for a long time. He was baptized about fifteen years ago.

Concerning the people he has associated with he asked to be excused, in order not to bring them into the same troubles in which he is, but he is willing to tell everything possible about himself. Asked whether he knows Pauwels Galle, he says not to his knowledge.

Would be willing to change his mind if he were convinced of something better on the basis of the truth.

At the same time in the Chamber:

Herman Vlecwijk stands by his first examination. He resided in Oudenburg by the sign of the ring. Says he is of the baptizers' faith. About seven or eight years ago he was imprisoned with several others from the city of Bruges and released without penalty because then he did not believe, but since then the

---

32 The designation "Scripture-minded" (scrifts-ghezint) appears just as often in these texts as a label for the Mennonites as does "baptism-minded" (doops-ghezint, to our day the name borne by the Dutch Mennonites is Doopsgezinde).

Spirit of God has taught him. After his release he attended secret meetings in the city of Bruges, but he asks to be excused from telling about it, not wanting to endanger anyone but himself.

Has attended the same kind of meetings in Germany and the country of Cleve.

The meetings were held in the woods, sometimes near St. Andries, outside Bruges, but it was a long time ago, well before the time of the [Calvinist] preaching [1566].

Attended a baptism at Ghent, which took place by day, but cannot tell the place. There were six or eight present. The name of the baptizer was Jan; he, Herman, was also baptized. He [Jan] was a man with a small beard, probably somewhat older than Herman; maybe about seven years ago.

Asked whether he saw anyone of his sect today, he answers that he does not know. He does not know whether anyone made signs to him, but only that someone called to him, but he did not see him and does not know who it was.[33]

Interrogation of Jacques de Rore, born at Courtrai, also named Squinting Coppen and among the Anabaptists Jacques the Candlemaker.

In the Chamber, May 11, 1569.[34]
What he is called among the Anabaptists.
Says that they call him Jacques the Candlemaker, because his father was a chandler.
How long have they considered him a preacher?
Says he has been a deacon for about six or seven years, but has not been a teacher. Was made a deacon[35] at Armentieres. Those who ordained him have been scattered. To be a deacon means to serve the poor.
Where has he lived most? Meenen, Wervik, Courtrai, Poperinge and thereabouts?
Has lived at Meenen, but had no trouble there. Has been at Poperinge, but that was long ago.
Did he preach in the fields around Meenen?
Admits having preached in the field and elsewhere around Meenen, two or three years ago.
Does he know Master Jacob 't Santele, pastor at Courtrai? During the Revolution did he go to him to invite him to debate?
Has heard tell of Master Jacob, but does not know him and never desired to debate with him.
Did he know Franchois Timmerman, obstinate heretic, executed six years ago at Courtrai, rebaptized at night at Courtrai?
Did not know Franchois Timmerman.
What about the teachers of his sect?

---

33 Marginal note (fol. 9vo): "On April 27, 1569, it was resolved to proceed to torture Jacob de Rore and Herman Vlecwijk, in order to learn where the conventicles were held, who was present, what they did, who has been rebaptized, and other things. However, since the executioner was not in town, they could not proceed against them the same day."

34 In the original document the questions form a column on the right, answers on the left.

35 The term here translated "deacon" is *vorstaender.*

Knows of no one in the country at present. Knows Joachim Sukerbacker, who is abroad, but he does not know where, and also a Joos from Holland; Joachim ordained him as deacon.

Does he know Gillis the Baptizer?

Knows no one by that name; knows a Gillis, but he has never been here.

Lucas the Hollander?

He knew him, but he died.

Paul the Baptizer?

Doesn't know him.

Dierick de Kethelaere?

Knows him, but does not know where he is.

Matthew from Nukerke?

Knows some persons from Nukerke named Matthew.

Who are the protectors in their church?[36]

Knows no such people.

Who are the almoners and other officers?

They are all scattered.

Does he know Antheunis de Vyl, Anabaptist executed at Courtrai in 1553?

Does not know him.

Does he know Hans van der Mote, repentant [i.e., apostate] Anabaptist rebaptized in a wood near Ypres about 1561, by one Joachim who celebrated the Lord's Supper there with about forty people, where Squinting Coppen or the Candlemaker was one of the ministers of the congregation, who call the congregation to the meetings?[37]

Does not know him. Knows Joachim, but did not know that he had even been near Ypres.

What exhortation or sermon did he preach between Rijsel and Meenen in a wood and at various other places?

Knows nothing about it.

Heindrick de Cock, of Thielt, repentant, says that Coppen preached an exhortation or a sermon when he, Heindrick, married Jaenken Hobbets after their fashion and that the same Coppen had told him where the meeting would be held.

He admits it. Heindrick was working for him. Heindrick married near Armentieres and Jacques knows nothing but that the woman's name was Jaenken. Affirms that he preached and that he married them. Those who attended the wedding would be hard to find, for it was about four or five years ago and at night.

Did he preach near Beselaere and in Keeselbosch?

Cannot remember.

---

36 It is not clear whether "protectors" *(beschoeders)* refers to some sentinel's function which the questioners thought to exist in the Mennonite churches, or to non-Mennonite friends who helped them to avoid capture.

37 Cf. note 35 above. This function is sometimes referred to as *vorstaender* (presider), sometimes as *weetdoener* (messenger); here it is described by a whole phrase. Jacques seems to have had this office in his home country around Armentières, but this testimony would seem to indicate that he was not thereby automatically empowered to function as leader of the Bruges group.

Or near Wervik in the fields?

Does not know.

Franchois Maertins, son of Dierix van Lendeley, repentant Anabaptist, says that Coppen took him to the place where he was baptized and that Coppen was regarded as one of the leaders of the Anabaptists and one of the best in explaining Scripture. Franchois himself heard him doing it.

Believes [Franchois] gave in to the inquisitor; is not sure of his name, but it may have been Lendeley.

Betkin van Wemelburch from Courtrai, repentant Anabaptist, says that Coppen attended the meeting at Courtrai where she was rebaptized in about 1556, and twelve others were baptized with her by Leenaert Bouwens.

Does not know her, but used to know Leenaert Bouwens. Does not know where he is. He has been outside the country a long time.

Tryskin van Male, repentant Anabaptist, has seen Coppen at meetings.

Knows no one by that name.

Daneel Vaercampt of Courtrai, obstinate Anabaptist, burned, had heard the preaching of Coppen near Roeselaere and elsewhere from 1551 or 1552 on.

Knows him; he was executed at Courtrai. They grew up together. This Daneel did not hear his preaching, for he was more learned than Jacques.

Pieter de Schippere, repentant, tells that Coppen has been Anabaptist for over thirteen years.

Does not know him.

Jacob van Kelsbeck has heard him preaching and says that Coppen had a child which was not baptized for a long time.

Died long ago of sickness: believes he gave in to the inquisitor.

How many marriages did he perform among the Anabaptists?

Does not remember.

Has he been at Courtrai, Meenen, Wervik, Roeselaere, Ypres, Thielt, the various quarters of Ghent, Armentieres, and Bruges?

Has been in these places.

Where is his wife; how many children does he have, and how many unbaptized?

Does not know where his wife is; married her near Armentieres in the midst of the congregation.

One Adriaen, since executed at Armentieres, preached. This was about ten years ago. Had six children, the eldest about seven or eight years old. His children have been baptized in the [Catholic] church. Three boys and two girls are living. Left his wife at Meenen.

Does he know Jan or Hanskin the Weaver, from Dadizele, for a long time minister and baptizer in these countries and a teacher, having led astray many young and old people? Which meetings did he hold and where did he celebrate the Lord's Supper?

Is abroad; was a minister and teacher. Knows that Hanskin celebrated the Lord's Supper; does not remember where, perhaps near Armentieres.

Does he know Pauwels de Backere, from Thielt, preacher, minister, and deacon in their sect, who does and has done much harm for a long time in leading people astray?

Knows him, but does not know where he is; perhaps abroad; for a long time he had no steady residence.

Who else besides those already known by the denunciations of other prisoners and other information has been baptized by Pauwels and Jacques?

Does not know whom Pauwels rebaptized and as for himself he has baptized no one; he is not authorized.

Leon Callinck, repentant Anabaptist, reports that Jacques preached near Wervik to forty or fifty people. Also all night long near de Cleppe; also in the Erckegem woods, in the woods near Waasten and Nijpkerke, and in a farm nearby. He also brought Leon to the place where he was baptized. Has preached in the meadows near Armentieres, between Meenen and Roeselaere, all night long. Also near Armentieres in the Hamme meadow, where twenty or twenty-five persons were present. Also near Armentieres on the road to Utrecht in a small meadow, where Karel Simoentz from Roeselaere, who lived with Jacques, was married.

Does not know Leon Callinck; confesses that he has taught near Wervik. He may have been near de Cleppe. Does not know whether he was in the Erckegem woods. He may have been in the woods of Waasten and also near Nijpkerke about two years ago; does not know who was present there. Has taught in the meadows near Armentieres, but does not know how long ago. Does not know the Hamme meadow.

Knows Karel Simoentz, who married at the meeting, for he himself preached there by night. Does not know how long ago it was; Karel lived with him, but he does not know Karel's wife's name.

Who are the women he took into his house, where they gave birth to children, which they did not baptize? Did he send his young wife away to have her child?

Maybe there were some women in his house to give birth to children, but will not name them. Asks that they leave him in peace about his wife.

Which Anabaptists did he lodge at his house, etc.?

Joachim has long been at home in Armentieres; at Bruges no one stayed in his house.

In the Chamber, May 12, 1569.

Jacques de Rore, interrogated about what happened here at Bruges during the two or three years that he has been living at Bruges, concerning his religion and those who are of like mind with him. Says that he knows nothing about it and that his companions are mostly scattered or dead. Nor can he name the places.

At his home there has never been any meeting. There have been meetings at the home of Maillaert de Grave, who was executed here; it was across the Flemish bridge, but he cannot name the street. It was in the winter about a year ago and he was a cabinetmaker. Jacques preached there, but not much; there was also a Jan de Cammere who was executed at Bruges.

Says he also attended meetings outside the city, and preached once or twice outside the Smede Gate, near St. Andries, where the same people were who were also at the night meeting.

There was also a Jan, born at Bruges, but he thinks he moved away. He has not been at Herman's house for such purposes. Has celebrated no marriages here and does not know of any baptism or Lord's Supper or such things held here. Says that he knows no one in the neighborhood of Oudenburg where he lived who was of his sect. At the meetings there was also a Gillis, executed at Bruges, and others who are scattered or dead and whom he cannot name.

There was a Jan and a Maillaert who knew him. Who were the women who were at his house for childbirth? Says he does not know and he did not send his wife elsewhere to give birth to her child. At his home there was one woman named Proonkin, from Waasten or thereabouts, whose husband's name is Leon; he does not know where the child is. As far as he knows it was baptized afterward; knows of no other women; at that time he was living in Armentieres.

In the Chamber at the same time.

Herman Vleckwijk, from Kervendonck, asked about his accomplices at Bruges and vicinity, answers that he knows no one and thinks most of them have been scattered and he himself had left and only returned to the city to straighten out his business.

Has been at meetings outside the city. Has peddled needles in the country westward to Rijsel and thereabouts, where he slept in several hostels.

At the meetings there was a certain Jan and a Lauken, surnames unknown, who are dead. On the lists in Bruges he is named Jan van der Cammen. Jan [was executed] with the sword and Lauken burned. Asked whether he has been at meetings where Jacques de Rore taught, he answers that he does not wish to speak about that.

Knows a certain Pietere, chairmaker, living in Oudenburch, but he is not of like mind with Herman. Herman has lived in " 't bosken" on Steen Street; knows no one named Michiel in " 't Genthof." Says afterward that his [Michiel's] wife always liked to buy from him [Herman]. But he has not seen him for a long time and was never in his house, nor does he know where he is.

The same time, under torture.

Herman Vleckwijk, asked where and when he has been to meetings where Jacques de Rore taught, says that he does not wish to say. He wishes to say only what concerns himself. Has been at Jan de Cammere's meeting. Says that Jacques is no teacher and that there is no deacon at Bruges.[38] He has five living children, which are at Cologne: the eldest is about twelve years old. His sons were baptized at Bruges and two of them are still unbaptized. His wife gave birth to those two here in Bruges in the Oudenburch; women of their sect assisted his wife; one of them was named Proonkin; when his wife gave birth to the last child they lived in the back of a house here in town, but he is silent concerning who lived in the front and where the house was, saying that those people are gone and live in the country of Cleve.[39]

In the Chamber the same day, afternoon.

Jacques de Rore, asked whether he has been in " 't bonte peert" on the Friday Market Square here in the city, says he cannot tell whether he was there. Has known a certain Clement; says that he was a Frenchman and does not know his surname; it may have been Clement Durant and does not know where he is now. About a month or six weeks ago he saw him in Gelderland.

38 Cf. note 37.

39 Marginal note (fol. 19): "Resolved to execute Herman Vlecwijk by fire. Done as above ordered. J. Damme. That he be strangled and his body hanged on a gallows."

When Jacques arrived in this city he first lived at the hostels "in den Bog-haert" and "in de drie Muenicken."

When he preached and taught near the new cloister, he did not know who or how many people were present. Asked where Herman has lived, he says on Steen Street. Asked where else, he says that Herman should be asked, for he, Jacques, has no knowledge thereof. Asked whether he knows where Herman lived in the back part of a house, says they should ask Herman, who is old and wise enough to answer concerning himself.

In the Castle of Bruges, by authorization of Milords of the Council, May 12, 1569, by Sir Charles van Boneem and Jan van Overschelde, Council members, in the presence of Achilles, on behalf of Milords.

Herman Vleckwijk, asked in what house he lived in the city of Bruges, says he has lived next to Jan Frays in the Oudenburch, in the corner house, where he had a shop. Has forgotten how long ago that was. Earlier he lived behind the house opposite St. Anteunis. Also in the house where Pietere van den Scelstraete, chairmaker, now lives, where he also had a shop. Afterward he lived in " 't bos-ken" on Steen Street and had a shop there too; moved away from there because he was being looked for by the police and went to live in a room "in den Zant-berg" on Welle Street; there also they came after him.

Shortly afterward he left the city. Denies having lived with his father-in-law in the back of a house, but they all lived together in " 't bosken." Denies having lived in a house behind Bellechiers, but Jacques de Rore lived there. The owner of the house was Franchois Schede.

Denies that his wife had children in that house. She had a child in the house where the smith lives, opposite Frays. It has not been baptized. He prefers not to tell where his other children were born, asking to be left in peace about this matter. When his wife gave birth to her last child, it was in the house of people who know nothing about it.

This was because the birth was earlier than expected, so they could no longer move into another house. He asks to be excused from saying more about the matter.

The same day, afternoon; absent, Achilles de Boom.

Herman Vleckwijk declares that his wife gave birth to her last child, a boy, unbaptized, at the house of Jacques Francq, a tailor, living at that time above the Strobridge along the Reye; afterward he left Bruges with his family to start a business in the county of Cleve. As soon as this Jacques knew to what sect Herman belonged, he told him to leave his house, which he did as soon as possible. However, the child was born earlier than Herman or his wife had expected; as soon as his wife had recovered he left the house with her and his children.

In the Chamber, June 8, 1569, forenoon.

Jacques de Rore, asked where he went to ask about lodging when he arrived in Bruges, says, to Jan de Cammere, who was executed here by Milords of Bruges. Asked who was present at the meetings which he attended, and who heard him, inside as well as outside the city of Bruges, he says that they are not to be found any more and are all scattered and besides it would not be accept-able to his conscience to bring anyone else trouble.[40]

---

[40] Marginal note (fol. 22vo): "June 8, 1569, resolved to execute by fire. Done as above ordered."

At the same time, under torture.

Jacques de Rore, asked which people were present at St. Andries when he preached there, says he cannot name them all; they are scattered and he cannot tell well, since it occurred at night and he has bad eyes. Jan de Cammere was present and was the one who convoked the people; he cannot name those who are still alive, since they were scattered since then. Asked whether he knows anyone else, says that he can name no one, nor does he know anyone's place of residence.[41]

13. Cost what it may, Gillis de Bruyckere must be captured, to explain the letters sent him by the brethren in Zeeland. June 20, 1573.[42]

The same day the bailiff was again ordered by Milords to do everything possible to arrest Gillis de Bruyckere, living on the Ledertauwers Canal, because of the letters, addressed to him, which came from Rassen a few days ago, on which the seal of the Mennonite congregation appears to be imprinted; entrusted by the secretary Eechaute to the bailiff.

If Bruyckere must be brought from his house by force, the Council will send the bailiff two of their men to assist him.[43]

14. Fierin Grysperre before the Calvinist government, July, 1583.[44]

Done in the Council of Milords on July 19, 1583.

Fierin Grysperre, from Hemelgem near Yseghem, weaver by trade, living in a shed behind the lime kiln, one of the heirs of Franchois van Sare, asked whether he confesses having written these things, says that he wrote them to bring to light the truth, which is God's Word, which he, Fierin, wishes to proclaim. He admits authorship of the notes which he posted at many places to that end.

He has also sometimes read one or two chapters from the Holy Scriptures in the presence of two, three, or more people at several places in this city and chiefly in the barn in which he lives, as well as "in den Zeehondt," the home of Pieter van Ooteghem near Gelmunte.

When asked what is the main emphasis of those who teach Menno's faith, says that he thinks their teachers have proclaimed the truth, lived it, and sealed it with life, goods, and blood. Says he does not represent Menno's teaching, but there were some Menno-minded among those who heard his preaching.[45] Asked where he entered the church of the Mennonists, says that it was in this city and that he was also baptized here. He is cut off from them because he refused to submit to their understanding.

Asked whether he is married, he answers yes, but he is not living with his wife because he is cut off from those called Mennonites.

Says that he was baptized by the elder or bishop of their congregation, Jan de Weert, who he thinks lives in Antwerp; is unwilling to tell in whose house in the city he was baptized.

41 Margin (fol. 22vo): "Give him gunpowder and hang the body on a gallows."
42 Ghent City, KR, 1571-74, fol. 192.
43 Margin: "Bailiff ordered to arrest Gillis de Bruyckere."
44 Ghent City, Crime, 1581-83, fol. 172.
45 Translator's note: This is the first of our sources to name Menno. Earlier appearances in the text of the term "Mennonite" have been as a translation of the Dutch "doopsgezind."

Feels himself impelled by God's Word to proclaim at the Hoye the proclamation or preaching which he has written down, and which he thinks is pure teaching of Menno, which he cannot, on the basis of Scripture, see to be anything but the exact truth.

Confesses that he does not stand watch but he gives money, and thinks it sufficient that he pays for the shot and lets the authorities do with it what they will.

Has been banned from his wife since September 30, 1582. Had he been banned for reasons found in God's Word he would have accepted it. But because he has not been banned in the presence of all the brethren and sisters of the church, he had let them know that he would post these notes and that he would prove that he had been banned unjustly, and would demand, as said before, that he be heard before all the brethren and sisters, since he had been banned by only a few of them and not in the presence of all the brethren.[46]

15. The Secret Council esteems that the nine Mennonites arrested at Ghent do not come into consideration for release because they continued to preach. May, 1585.[47]

To His Highness,
Sire,

In conformity to Your Highness' letters of the second of the month we have reviewed and examined the problem of the government of the city of Ghent, concerning the nine Anabaptists arrested by them, as well as the three points concerning which they consulted Your Highness, together with the advice of the Council of Flanders.

To express also our opinion on the first point, following what it has pleased Your Highness to communicate to us: it seems to us, Sire, subject to your correction, that seeing the general character of the Fourth Article of the Treaty of Reconciliation of Ghent, there is no reason to maintain that the Anabaptists are less included in the terms thereof than are the Calvinists and other sectarians, who are no less pernicious, but even more seditious, violent, turbulent, and dangerous than said Anabaptists. Nevertheless, since the earlier the city of Ghent is purged of all kinds of sects and heresies, the better it will fare and the safer it will be, we would judge appropriate the use of an oath, required by the Council of Flanders, which would give one grounds to expel the recalcitrants, if it should seem to Your Highness that the present state of affairs in the city and the times allow it.

On the second point we are of the opinion that these prisoners should not for their part enjoy the privileges of the treaty, because they have, in contradiction to its terms, created scandal by the meetings held since then. They not only have collected money for the support of their members, but also taught and preached after their manner, as is made evident by the express confession of Pierre Gazebaert, one of said prisoners, which is also not denied by the other Anabaptists, who only refuse to answer.

Consequently (which will serve as our opinion on the third point) Your

---

46 Two marginal notes: "Resolves to put in prison. Done July 19, 1583." "Council bans Fierin Grysperre from this city for three years, forbidding him to enter the city meanwhile, under pain of summary punishment."

47 Brussels Royal, *Geheime (Spaansche Beurnid)*, No. 1117 (original in French).

Highness will do well to instruct Milords of Ghent to investigate more closely said assemblies, by torture or otherwise, to know who are their accomplices and leaders, and what they do in their meetings. This seems to be the subject of an extract of a manual which was found on the prisoners and which we enclose: and having learned this, to proceed against them as transgressors and disturbers of public order, under such penalty as is advised by the Council of Flanders as sovereign judicial authority in the province, who shall decide how to proceed. We, however, lay the whole question before the very wise discretion of Your Highness, to whom we return all the documents concerning the matter, to be disposed of according to the good pleasure of Your Highness.

Kissing most humbly the hands of Your Highness, we pray the Creator that He will keep him for a long and prosperous life.

At Tournai, May 13, 1585.

16. Interrogation of Michiel de Cleercq; Ghent, July, 1592.[48]

July 1, 1592, in the Castle, in the presence of Sir Franchois and Jacques Borluyt.

Michiel de Cleercq, son of Jan, forty years old or so, born at St. Hentelins [St. Antelinks] in the country of Aalst, weaver by trade, responds that he has lived here in the city continually in different houses and streets, moving from one to the other to avoid suspicion and arrest by the pastors and the police, for about eleven years: outside the Braem Gate "in de Keysere"; on Abeel Street about the time of the Reconciliation; and elsewhere. He, however, refuses to state where he lived afterward or where he lives now or for whom he has been working or with whom he has been in contact; further questioned on this matter, says they should be patient with him. Pressed further to answer more directly on such points, says that he will have to think longer, as he is not inclined now to say more. Says that last night, to escape the police, he had taken refuge in a rented room in the house of Dierick de Scryvere and had slept there.

Asked the purpose of the packages of money found in the possession of Reineux Pantens, says he knows nothing about it.

Says he knows Franchois Hubrecht, called Lochtenier, living outside the city, supporting himself by buying yarn. Is not willing to name the village or region.

Confesses that he left and denied the Roman Catholic Church in the beginning of the recent troubles and adhered to the Calvinistic sect; but after having been further instructed, he decided that this was not the true faith either, and once again abandoned and denied it in favor of the faith of the Anabaptists, which he tested and adopted as the true faith, in which he wants to stand fast forever, notwithstanding the fact that he was baptized in the Holy Roman Catholic Church. He holds such a baptism to be null and void, so that, repudiating it, and in violation of the promise made thereby, he had himself baptized together with several others by a minister of this sect about four years ago in this city in the house "den Reghenboghe" on the Pas, where at that time there lived a certain widow, named Mayken, who has since left the city. He refuses to name the minister or those present. Afterward says that Reineux Pantens, with several others whom he will not name, was present. Asked to whom the goods belong which

48 Ghent City, *Crime*, 1591-94, fol. 56 ff.

were found in his room, as well as the goods which he brought yesterday to his room in Dierick de Schryvere's house, assisted by a certain woman, and who the woman is who helped him, says that he will not answer these questions or name anyone; he also says that there are some goods in his room which are his own property, namely, among other things, six pounds of unbleached yarn.